HACKNEY LIBRARY SERVICES *A*

Please return this book to any library in Hackney, on or
before the last date stamped. Fines may be charged if it is late.
Avoid fines by renewing the book (subject to it NOT being reserved).

Call the renewals line on 020 8356 2539

People who are over 60, under 18 or registered disabled
are not charged fines.

DO'S & DON'TS

An Anthology of Forgotten
Manners

Rosemary Hawthorne

PAVILION

Dedicated to all those who still use asparagus tongs

Rosemary Hawthorne is a fashion and social historian and the author of *Knickers: an Intimate Appraisal, Bras: a Private View* and *Stockings and Suspenders: a Quick Flash.* She is married to a clergyman, they have seven children and live in Gloucestershire.

First published in Great Britain in 1997 by
PAVILION BOOKS LIMITED
26 Upper Ground
London SE1 9PD

General introduction and chapter introductions © Rosemary Hawthorne 1997
Quotations selected by Rosemary Hawthorne

Cover designed by Elizabeth Ayer
Text designed by Penny Mills

The moral right of the author has been asserted.

A CIP catalogue record for this book is available from the British Library

ISBN 1 86205 012 0

Printed and bound in Finland by WSOY

2 4 6 8 10 9 7 5 3 1

This book may be ordered by post direct from the publisher.
Please contact the Marketing Department.
But try your bookshop first.

Picture Acknowledgements
Cover and page 1 © Mary Evans Picture Library.
All other illustrations courtesy of Rosemary Hawthorne's private collection.

Contents

Introduction

WHEN WE THINK of 'Manners' it's possible we put them in an old-fashioned setting — they seem to be something that happened *then*, not *now*. What are they and were there more of them in the old days and how were they 'applied'? For certain, before the late eighteenth century, and the beginning of the nineteenth century, the laws and rules governing personal behaviour — or etiquette (which originally meant 'ticket') — were handed down by example, one to another.

Correct, disciplined manners and customs, apart from being civilizing influences, are cultivated class 'distinguishers' used, then and now, as subliminal codes to select and attract the social group to which you, mainly by birth and nurture, belong. Thus manners, or lack of them, set you apart and, possibly, seal your fate in the stratagems of society. But, ideally, you don't put on manners, like an overcoat, when you go out to socialize — they should be inherently part of you.

In the nineteenth and early twentieth centuries, when these things truly mattered, this was all very well if you happened to have been born into the bosom of a seriously upper-class or middle-class family; the genetic code would have been in place and given off its signals, picking up returned messages as easily as breathing. But, what if Mother Nature, by some accident, had been neglectful or mismanaged on your behalf, and left you 'doing nicely' and wishing to spiral further towards the dizzy reaches of High Society without making a fool of yourself? Ah, then you had to learn a trick or two.

You would turn eagerly to some of the hundreds of self-educating books that were written and published once the peasants revolted. You would savour the tidbits on offer: you would rehearse how not to eat peas off your knife or slurp your soup; be informed as to what was worn at a boating party; know how to address a dowager duchess in mourning for her husband; and how not to mention money on the wrong occasions, if at all.

In other words, to acquire the confidence and charm of the gently bred, you became a student and, aided by the helpful 'Enquire Within' technique, memorized – or at least, brushed up – your manners.

Most of all, for those yearning for the style of 'a gentleman' or that of 'a lady', you would hope to acquire the secrets that allowed acceptance into the company of those you felt keen, or, frankly, needed, to join.

ROSEMARY HAWTHORNE
Tetbury Vicarage, 1997

CHAPTER I

Manners for Calling

Cards, Visiting, Receiving, Introductions, 'At Homes',
Court Presentation and Other Observances

THE FIRST STEP on the road to the Kingdom of Polite Society was possibly the most difficult. You had to cultivate and enlarge your circle of 'better class' acquaintance. For this the etiquette was accurate, rigorous, finely observed, and totally obscure. But, without this basic skill, you were a non-starter in the Good Society game. The rules had to be understood and acted upon — they were the passport without which the traveller could not proceed. It is not surprising that, from the early nineteenth century, the latent rituals were aimed, principally, at women — who, as ever, had the task of networking on behalf of their husbands and family.

Initially, the most important thing was the card. You might think this would be a simple matter? But, no, the visiting card was imbued with unforeseen 'oops' and made heavy with meaning. If a lady called and left a card with the upper-left corner folded over, this indicated 'felicitation', if it were the lower-left, it conveyed 'condolence'. The right-hand upper corner of a card implied that these emotions extended to the daughter or daughters of the house and if the whole right-hand side was folded back it betokened that this was brought in person, not dropped off by a servant. A gentleman never 'cornered' his card. The number of cards left was also significant.

As Lord Chatham said in the eighteenth century, 'Politeness is benevolence in trifles'. There was more to a card than a bit of pasteboard.

When driving, a lady should desire her footman to inquire if the mistress of the house at which she is calling is 'at home'. If not 'at home', and it is the first call, she should hand him three cards — one of her own, and two of her husband's. Her card is left for the mistress of the house, and her husband's cards are for both master and mistress.

Manners and Rules of Good Society (1912)

Nothing better shows the standing of ladies or gentlemen, or their familiarity with the usages of the best society, than the use of their cards. The quality of the card, its size and style, the hour and manner in which it is left — all these convey a silent message to the experienced eye which indicates the character of the caller.

Modern Manners and Social Forms
JULIA M. BRADLEY (1889)

Visiting Cards — The Proper Size. Three-and-a-half inches by two-and a-half is supposed to be the proper size for a lady's card, and three inches by one-and-a-half for a gentlemen's. There have been some slight variations in size, however, in ladies' cards of late, and their tendency is to become smaller and smaller. Small cards are more convenient to carry, but the old fashioned size looks the best style.

Etiquette-Up-To-Date
LUCIE HEATON ARMSTRONG (c.1924)

The thicker the card at the present moment the more secure you are in fashion's favour.

Home Chat (1895)

The card-case is an indispensable companion, for, should your friend be from home, it is only courteous to leave a card.

A Manual of Etiquette for Ladies (1855)

A married lady should never use her christian name on a card, but she should use her husband's christian name if his father or elder brother is living.

Manners and Rules of Good Society (1912)

A young lady being taken out by relatives ... does not carry her own cards, but her name is written in pencil under that of the lady chaperoning her.

Complete Etiquette for Ladies and Gentlemen (c.1920)

Leaving cards principally devolves upon the mistress of the house ... The master of a house has little or no card-leaving to do, beyond cards for his bachelor friends.

Manners and Rules of Good Society (1912)

CARD LEAVING DONE, the next stage involved an actual, physical response. Having affirmed via the servant that Mrs So and So is 'At home' as against 'Not at home' (when she might well be in residence but not receiving callers) then:

When bent on paying calls, first don one of your

prettiest gowns, then arm yourself with a liberal supply of small-talk and sally forth unafraid.

Etiquette for Women G.R.M. DEVEREUX (1902)

First visits to commence an acquaintance, are always paid by the person of the highest rank or social consideration.

Complete Etiquette for Ladies (1900)

Letters of introduction are to be regarded as tickets of respectability. In England ... called 'letter to soup' because it is customary to invite a gentleman to dine who comes with a letter of introduction to you.

Martine's Hand Book of Etiquette (1865)

A lady never calls on a gentleman, unless professionally or officially. It is not only ill-bred, but positively improper to do so.

The Habits of Good Society (c.1859)

In London, the limits of calling hours are fixed, namely, from three to six, but in the country people are sometimes odious enough to call in the morning before lunch.

The Habits of Good Society (c.1859)

If the visitor be a lady, she may remove her victorine [fur stole], but on no account either her shawl or bonnet, even if politely requested ... Some trouble is necessarily required in replacing them, and this ought to be avoided.

Martine's Hand Book of Etiquette (1865)

Morning visits should not be prolonged above half-an-hour ... and the visit should be made, not before eleven, and not after three o'clock.

A Manual of Etiquette for Ladies (1855)

Never look at your watch during a morning visit; it is very rude to do so.

Etiquette for Ladies and Gentlemen (c.1870)

Young ladies do not receive calls from gentlemen, unless they ... have passed the rubicon of thirty summers.

The Habits of Good Society (c.1859)

Courtseying is obsolete. Ladies now universally bow instead. The latter is certainly more convenient, ... especially on the street.

How to Be a Lady W. NICHOLSON (c.1880)

Many ladies adopt the plan of always being at home on stated afternoons, which are written on their visiting cards thus: 'At home on Thursdays'; 'At home the first and third Monday in the month'.

Cassell's Book of Etiquette (1921)

One must be careful if cards have been left, and no visit personally made, to follow suit, and to be sure to pay a visit, if a visit has been paid to you, within a week; nothing stamps one's status more than failure in these details.

Complete Etiquette for Ladies and Gentlemen (c.1920)

Morning calls (so designated because they are paid before dinner) are made between the hours of four and seven.

Complete Etiquette for Ladies (1900)

Punctuality is one of the characteristics of politeness.

Martine's Hand Book of Etiquette (1865)

Calling is guided by different rules in different places. In the country the resident calls first. In town the country cousin must take the initiative, or the Londoner will not know he has arrived.

Etiquette-Up-To-Date
LUCIE HEATON ARMSTRONG (c.1924)

Do not take a family party with you to call on a friend in town ... A family party can, however, pay a visit to a country house; it is quite good form to do so.

Complete Etiquette for Ladies and Gentlemen (c.1920)

Never take your pet dog when paying a call. Many persons have a great objection to animals.

Etiquette for Ladies and Gentlemen (c.1870)

It is not desirable to take either very small children or dogs when paying a call.

Cassell's Book of Etiquette (1921)

Presentation at Court: The wives and daughters of the clergy, of military and naval officers, of physicians and barristers, can be presented. The wives and daughters of merchants, or of men of business (excepting bankers), are not entitled to presentation. Nevertheless, though many ladies of this class were refused presentation early in this reign, it is certain that many have since been presented, whether by accident, or by a system of making the Queen more accessible.

The Habits of Good Society (1859)

A well-bred person always receives visitors ... but if you are occupied and cannot afford to be interrupted you should instruct the servant beforehand to say you are 'not at home'.

The Habits of Good Society (1859)

A 'bore' is a person who does not know when you have had enough of his or her company.

The Habits of Good Society (1859)

At large 'At Homes' the hostess remains, practically stationary, near the drawing-room door and guests entertain each other. During music they will be as silent as possible.

Complete Etiquette for Ladies and Gentlemen (c.1920)

The introduction is of an inferior (which position a gentleman always holds to a lady) to the superior.

The Habits of Good Society (1859)

An English duchess should be addressed as 'Duchess' by all persons conversing with her belonging to the upper classes, and as 'Your Grace' by all other classes.

Manners and Rules of Good Society (1912)

Money is never talked of in polite society; it is taken for granted.

The Book of Good Manners
MRS BURTON KINGSLAND (1901)

The etiquette of hand-shaking is simple. A man has no right to take a lady's hand till it is offered.

The Habits of Good Society (1859)

Ladies never shake hands with gentlemen unless under circumstances of great intimacy.

*The Standard Cyclopaedia of Useful Knowledge,
Vol. V*
ANON. (1896)

The gentleman who shakes hands with great warmth and empressement are two distinct individuals; the one is cordial and large-hearted — the other wishes to ingratiate himself.

Manners and Rules of Good Society (1912)

You need not stop to pull off your glove to shake hands … If it is warm weather it is more agreeable to both parties that the glove should be on — especially if it is a lady with whom you shake … as the perspiration of your bare hand would be very likely to soil her glove.

Martine's Hand Book of Etiquette (1865)

A sudden and complete silence should never follow an introduction.

Gems of Deportment ANON. (1880)

There are definitive rules for 'cutting'. A gentleman must never cut a lady under any circumstances. An unmarried lady should never cut a married one. A servant of whatever class should never cut his master; near relations should never cut one another at all; and clergymen should never cut anybody, because it is at best an un-christian action.

The Habits of Good Society (1859)

When in Company, put not your Hands to any Part of the Body, not usually Discovered.

George Washington's Rules of Civility and *Decent Behaviour in Company and Conversation* Edited by CHARLES MOORE (1747/1926)

CHAPTER II

Manners for Feasting

*Luncheon, Dinner, Large Teas, Picnics and
Other Refreshments*

H AVING ACQUIRED A circle of suitably classy
friends and been welcomed into their homes,
the next area of concern for a determined social
climber was eating.

The upper classes may all have started off as cave-
people with the rest of us, but what quickly marked them
out was the ease with which they mastered not only the
correct pecking order (later they relied on *Burke's
Peerage*) but being able to peck so impeccably.

> Pick not thy teeth at the table syttynge,
> Nor use at thy meate over much spyttynge.
>
> FRANCIS SEAGER, *The Schoole of Vertue* (1557)

Apart from who sat where, and never as one of thirteen, the past two hundred years have been beset by four Feasting Foes causing endless, nerve-wracked bewilderment; namely, pea-eating, artichokes, fish knives and table napkins. As the *Ladies' Manual of Etiquette* pointed out in 1855, 'Dining is an art.'

During the nineteenth century better class eating underwent certain changes of emphasis. Having emerged from the Dark Age of providing your own knife and spoon when you went to chomp at a friend's house (where you would have been provided with only one plate, for everything) the next moment, la!, there were neatly placed forks and a need for dainty manners in front of the ladies. The English became the bench-mark for those exquisite laws that governed the table ... but the Americans gave us lunch.

> Never use your knife to convey your food to your mouth, under any circumstances; it is unnecessary, and glaringly vulgar. Feed yourself with a fork or spoon, nothing else — a knife is only for cutting.
>
> *Hints on Etiquette* (1836)

> Eat peas with a dessert spoon; and curry also.
>
> *Hints on Etiquette* (1836)

> Soup should be eaten with a table-spoon and not a dessert-spoon, it would be out of place to use a dessert-

spoon for ... as their name implies, ... are intended for eating fruit-tarts, custard puddings, or any sweet not sufficiently substantial to be eaten with a fork.

Manners and Rules of Good Society (1912)

Luncheons have recently come into great prominence as a form of modern-day hospitality, and a decided boon they have proved to both hostess and guests.

Etiquette for Ladies (1900)

The dinner-hour varies from 7.45 (an hour which old-fashioned people like), 8 o'clock, 8.15 to 8.30, which is the fashionable hour.

The Book of Etiquette LADY TROUBRIDGE (1926)

In Town the usual hour for luncheon is 1-30 to 2 o'clock; in the country it is generally half an hour earlier.

Manners and Rules of Good Society (1912)

Outside of those who are busy men and those who are idle men, and therefore late risers, there is another semi-occupied class of men who are always amenable to an invitation to lunch.

Manners and Rules of Good Society (1912)

At a formal luncheon, a hostess would not wait more than a few minutes for a guest who was late; ... on arrival ... it is not considered necessary to bring back all the courses unless he arrives so late ... he would go unfed. People who give trouble of this kind, unless for excellent reason, are liable to find that they are not asked again.

The Book of Etiquette LADY TROUBRIDGE (1926)

Luncheon has always been considered rather in the light of a feminine meal, but it is only within the last few years that the harmless, necessary man has been done away with altogether.

Etiquette-Up-To-Date
LUCIE HEATON ARMSTRONG (c.1924)

Ladies do not remove their hats at lunch ... The hostess wears a smart indoor dress; it would not be correct for her to wear a hat ... in her own house.

Etiquette-Up-To-Date
LUCIE HEATON ARMSTRONG (c.1924)

If you are wearing wraps which you wish to discard ... hand them to the maid ... but you keep your hat on, and do not remove your gloves until sitting down to lunch.

Etiquette Up To Date
CONSTANCE BURLEIGH (1925)

As to the fashionable setting of the luncheon-table ... the all-covering white cloth is no longer essential ... high laundry charges of recent times have had much to do with reducing the use of table linen.

Cassell's Book of Etiquette (1921)

Given ... a table-cover and a white damask table-cloth over it, what are we to place thereon? First, nothing high enough to come between the heads of any two of the party, and therefore must epergnes, lamps, and so forth be eschewed as nuisances ... to be elegant, you may have two table-fountains.

The Habits of Good Society (1859)

The napkins may be folded according to fancy ... For my part, I prefer to think no hands have been soiling mine before I use it ... lay them on the table or plate just as they come from the washerwoman's.

The Habits of Good Society (1859)

At all times, over-elaboration in napkin folding is in bad taste, and should be avoided by all with a high standard in such matters. A great many consider it bad form to substitute the French word 'Serviette' ... In any case, it is advisable that attendants in public dining-rooms should use the English term, and so avoid the possibility of giving annoyance to those who dislike the word serviette. Such trifling things annoy many who are only too ready to complain.

The Art of the Table
C. HERMANN SENN, MBE, FRHS (1923)

First, there are some people whom you must invite sooner or later, namely, those at whose houses you have dined; because you may neglect every Christian duty, and be less blamed than if you omit this social one.

The Habits of Good Society (1859)

Dinner invitations must be answered at once. It is most inconsiderate to leave a hostess in uncertainty and unable to complete her party.

The Book of Etiquette LADY TROUBRIDGE (1926)

A dinner invitation, once accepted, is a sacred obligation. If you die before the dinner takes place, your executor must attend the dinner.

Society As I Have Found It
WARD MCALLISTER (1890)

Places of honour at the dinner party are those at the right hand and left hand of the master of the house, who generally is seated at the lowest end of the table, the lady occupying the head of the table.

A Manual of Etiquette for Ladies (1855)

The women remove their gloves and lay them in their laps. The habit of tucking them in at the wrists, or worse, placing them in a wineglass, is inelegant.

The Book of Good Manners
MRS BURTON KINGSLAND (1901)

It should be said that in some extremely modern houses the American habit of offering a 'cocktail' as the guests sit down to dinner has established itself.

Cassell's Book of Etiquette (1921)

In no well-regulated society does a man forget the

courtesy due to the opposite sex, and those attentions of
the dinner table, so slight but so important.

A Manual of Etiquette for Ladies (1855)

Never put your feet so far under the table as to touch
those of the person on the opposite side.

Manual of Social and Business Forms
THOMAS E. HILL (1882)

The dining-room must be, of course, carpeted even in
the heat of summer, to deaden the noise of the servants'
feet.

The Habits of Good Society (1859)

In dealing with bread, use neither knife nor fork. It
must be broken with the fingers.

Good Manners for All Occasions
MARGARET E. SANGSTER (1921)

I beg you will not make that odious noise when
drinking your soup. It is louder than a dog drinking
water ... Then you need not scrape up the plate in that
way, nor even tilt it to get the last drop. It is not the
custom to take two helpings, and ... to keep other
people waiting. But don't you hear the servant offering
you sherry? I wish you would attend, for my servants
have quite enough to do and can't wait all evening while
you finish that very mild story to Miss Goggles.

The Habits of Good Society (1859)

The rule is that one person cannot attend to more than six persons.

Cassell's Book of Etiquette (1921)

It was ... discovered that a steel knife gave an unpalatable flavour to the fish, and a crust of bread was substituted.

Manners and Rules of Good Society (1912)

Will you, or will you not do turbot? Ah, but that is no reason why you should take up the knife too. Fish, I repeat, must never be touched with a knife. Take a fork in the right and a small piece of bread in the left hand.

The Habits of Good Society (1859)

This fashion lasted a considerable time, in spite of the fingers being brought unpleasantly near ... One evening a well-known diner-out discarded his crust ... and ate his fish with two silver forks. This fashion had its little day (apart from Royalty) ... they were not altogether satisfactory, and were superseded.

Manners and Rules of Good Society (1912)

Fish is eaten with a silver knife and fork, instead of the old-fashioned plan of a fork aided by a piece of bread.

Etiquette for Ladies (1900)

Lord Byron was responsible for a great deal of affectation when he said he hated to see a woman eat.

The beauties of the day thought it was elegant to appear to eat nothing.

Etiquette-Up-To-Date
LUCIE HEATON ARMSTRONG (c.1924)

It should not be necessary to mention that peas are gently pressed on to the fork with the knife and thus conveyed to the mouth, never by means of a spoon or knife!

Etiquette Up To Date
CONSTANCE BURLEIGH (1925)

Artichokes are, it may be said, an awkward and untidy vegetable ...; the outside leaves should be removed with the knife and fork, and the inner leaves which surround the heart, ... conveyed to the mouth with the fingers and sucked dry; ... at dinner-parties young ladies should not attempt to eat these.

Manners and Rules of Good Society (1912)

Asparagus may also be eaten with the fingers, except if it is very young and flabby, in which case it is better to eat it with a fork.

Etiquette-Up-To-Date
LUCIE HEATON ARMSTRONG (c.1924)

If small asparagus tongs are provided they are used instead of the fingers.

Etiquette Up To Date
CONSTANCE BURLEIGH (1925)

When eating grapes, the half-closed hand should be placed to the lips, and the stones and skins adroitly allowed to fall into the fingers and quickly placed on the side of the plate, the back of the hand concealing the manoeuvre from view.

The Manners and Tone of Good Society
BY A MEMBER OF THE ARISTOCRACY (1895)

The finger-glasses are not intended for you to wet your napkin in, and wipe your mouth, but simply to put your fingers in before wiping them on a napkin.

A Manual of Etiquette for Ladies (1855)

When the cloth is removed, and the decanters introduced, it is the signal for the ladies to retire. In due time, now a very much shorter time than formerly, the gentlemen join them in the drawing-room.

A Manual of Etiquette for Ladies (1855)

On rising from the table, the table-napkin must not be folded, but just put down on the table or chair.

The Book of Etiquette LADY TROUBRIDGE (1926)

Plates and d'oyleys are *not* used in good society at 'afternoon tea'; to use them would be considered 'bad style'. Equally *so* would it be to envelop the teapot in a wrap or cap known as a 'tea cosy'; a thing which should never be seen in a lady's drawing room.

Manners and Tone of Good Society
BY A MEMBER OF THE ARISTOCRACY (1895)

Tea is served under ordinary circumstances to any visitors between 4 and 5 o'clock. On an At Home day, the present custom is to have a table laid ... with the cups and saucers and the cakes, and let one or more of the maids stand behind it and dispense the tea. This should be done whenever possible from pots, not urns, for in the latter the tea becomes overdrawn and contains the undesirable tannic acid.

The favourite cakes are those contained in little paper cups, as these can be eaten without fear of injuring the gloves.

Cassell's Book of Etiquette (1921)

Picnics by Motor Car and Picnics by Rail: When a picnic party is to proceed to its destination by rail, a saloon carriage is engaged beforehand, an arrangement is made at the nearest hotel to supply the party with luncheon from 5s. to 10s. per head; or hampers of provisions are taken under the charge of one or two men-servants. If the picnic party proceeds by road, a coach is the favourite mode of conveyance.

Cassell's Book of Etiquette (1921)

Lastly, as to picnics, they are no longer the cheery gatherings of other days, when each person brought his quantum ... The only thing you are asked to bring in the present day is your very best spirits; and everybody is expected to contribute to these, for you cannot have too much of them.

The Habits of Good Society (1859)

Breakfast is a more or less moveable feast, especially in large households ... Hot dishes are placed at one end of the table opposite the master ... The other end is generally occupied with the ... tea and coffee equipage. The many cereal preparations, which principally hail from America, and which are becoming increasingly popular in English households, are usually served first as appetizers, either cooked, or au naturel, to be followed by the more substantial dishes of meat and fish. Upon the table is also placed in orderly array various necessary items, such as plates of rolls, racks of toast, butter, glasses of jam or marmalade, and fruit, which, when eaten raw, is considered far more digestible if eaten at breakfast rather than any later in the day.

The Art of the Table
C. HERMANN SENN, MBE, FRHS (1923)

But, stop, I had nearly forgotten Grace. Well, that is nothing very extraordinary, for the thanksgiving is positively the last thought of the diner, and when it is remembered, it is too often reduced to a mere formality.

The Habits of Good Society (1859)

CHAPTER III

Manners for Dressing

*Seemliness, Good Taste, Eccentricity and Other
Improprieties*

THE COMPLEXITIES CONCERNING do's and don'ts in dress became more and more critical during the nineteenth century as the previously 'have not's ... quite' began to encroach onto the territory of the 'have's ... always'. Distinctions had to be made. The upper-classes fine-fenced their sartorial boundaries to keep out trespassers and appear to have developed an obsession with gloves. Most of all, polite society shuddered at any sign of 'show', defining the 'latest fashion' as parvenu and flashy. New clothes, like new furniture, singled you out as wishing to be conspicuous and for those seeking help along their social way this was a particular enemy to guard against. The quest for unimpeachable dress was elusive, needing an ability to merge without remark and yet still retain distinguishing style.

This was a cunning that defeated many enthusiastic new socialites.

Two formidable bastions of correct dress, Weddings and Funerals, and the lesser rituals of Balls (as in dancing) and Sport, will be dealt with under appropriate chapters.

> Be not the first by whom the new is tried,
> Nor yet the last by whom 'tis set aside.

The Complete Etiquette for Gentlemen (c.1878)

> Propriety is outraged when a man of sixty dresses like a youth of sixteen.

Etiquette for Ladies and Gentlemen (c.1870)

A gentleman will always be well and tastefully dressed – choosing a sort of middle course between … avoiding foppery on the one hand, and carelessness on the other. Upon this subject the ladies are the only infallible oracles.

> *The Young Man's Companion.* Based on the works compiled by EDWARD TURNER (1866)

Wadding or stuffing should be avoided as much as possible. A little may be judiciously used to round off the more salient points of an angular figure, but when it is used for the purpose of creating an egregiously false impression of superior form, it is simply snobbish.

> *The Complete Etiquette for Gentlemen* (c.1878)

A woman of simple habits, accompanied with nicety and good taste, rarely goes wrong; at any rate is rarely supposed to do so.

> *The Habits of Good Society* (1859)

It is left for people out of the polite circle to dazzle the eyes of their friends and bewilder their acquaintances by gorgeous attire.

> *A Manual of Etiquette for Ladies* (1855)

Don't wear a fine gown and shabby boots: to do so stamps a woman at once.

> *Etiquette for Women* G.R.M. DEVEREUX (1919)

To be fancifully dressed, in gaudy colours, is to be very badly dressed ... and is an example of ill taste which is rarely met with among people of substantial good breeding.

How to be a Lady W. NICHOLSON (c.1880)

Every women should, habitually, make the best of herself.

The Habits of Good Society (1859)

The over-showy dress at a restaurant has always an air of being worn there because its possessor has nowhere else to display it.

Cassell's Book of Etiquette (1921)

Your dress should be consistent with your age and your natural exterior. However ugly you may be, rest assured that there is some style of dress which will make you passable.

The Young Man's Companion. Based on the works compiled by EDWARD TURNER (1866)

Ladies of a swarthy complexion should on no account attempt blues, lavenders or any other violent colours.

A Manual of Etiquette for Ladies (1855)

Ladies who have long passed the age of youth ought to avoid the adoption of any new fashion.

How to be a Lady W. NICHOLSON (c.1880)

Sky-blue and pea-green are the most trying colours that can be worn.

A Manual of Etiquette for Ladies (1855)

Gloves are a matter of extreme importance. They afford an elegant finish ... to costume, which cannot be omitted.

A Manual of Etiquette for Ladies (1855)

Men should wear gloves in the street, or at a ball; when paying a call, driving, riding, and in church; but not usually in the country, unless they are strong and useful.

Cassell's Book of Etiquette (1921)

A gentleman faultlessly gloved cannot go far wrong.

Social Etiquette MAUD C. COOKE (186–)

Old gloves with the tips of the fingers cut off should be worn when employed in any occupation likely to stain the hands.

Etiquette for Ladies and Gentlemen (c.1870)

Gloves should be worn by ladies in church, and in places of public amusement.

How to be a Lady W. NICHOLSON (c.1880)

Among the fopperies that a gentleman may permit himself, that of a white hat-lining is most excusable – though to preserve it free from taint it must be constantly renewed.

Etiquette for Ladies and Gentlemen (c.1870)

A hat should never be worn on going into church. Remove it in the vestibule, and on no account resume it until you return thither, unless health imperatively demands your doing so just before reaching the door.

The Complete Etiquette for Gentlemen (c.1878)

Having entered the house, take up with you to the drawing-room both hat and cane, but leave an umbrella in the hall.

The Habits of Good Society (1859)

On Presentation at Court: Only full dress (low bodice and short sleeves) is admissible, and those ladies who from ill-health are compelled to wear high dresses are required to obtain permission from the Lord Chamberlain's office ... A Court train is also de rigueur, and should be from three to four yards long.

Etiquette for Ladies (1900)

The hair ... when it is rich and full, a very slight head-dress of Mechlin or Lisle lace, for married women, ... is becoming; when thin and weak, a cap should be worn with a ribbon coming down infront. Nothing looks so bad as thin hair, underneath which the head is discernible in the day-time.

The Habits of Good Society (1859)

The bonnet may either be as simple as possible, or as rich; but it must not encroach upon that to be worn at a fete, a flower show or a morning concert.

The Habits of Good Society (1859)

Delicate and fragile people should wear light colours and transparent textures.

Etiquette for Ladies and Gentlemen (c.1870)

In France, the high dress is still worn at dinners, even those of full dress. In England, that custom ... never becomes general; there is no doubt that a low dress is by far the most becoming, according to age, complexion, and style of the house — a point not always taken into consideration. Yet I should restrict this to dinners by candle-light. In summer a thin high dress, at any rate, is more convenient and more modest. Since there is something in exposing the bare shoulders and arms to the glare of day, that startles the observer.

The Habits of Good Society (1859)

The low-necked dress is a fatal lure to many a woman who ought to know better than to display her physical imperfections to the gaze of a pitiless world.

Our Manners and Social Customs
DAPHNE DALE (1891)

Where pearl powder has been made an article of habitual use, wrinkles soon require additional layers to fill it up, just as worn out roads have ruts, and must be repaired; but the macadamizing process cannot be applied to wrinkles.

The Habits of Good Society (1859)

At large dinners, diamonds may be worn, but only in a brooch, or pendant from the throat; a full suite of diamonds is suitable to very full dress alone. The same rule applies to emeralds but not pearls. Rows of pearls, confined by a diamond snap, are beautiful in every dress.

The Habits of Good Society (1859)

Jewels are an ornament to women, but a blemish to men ... a man of good taste will wear as little jewellery as possible. Let all have some use. A handsome signet-ring on the little finger of the left-hand, a scarf-pin ... and a rather thin watch-guard ... the plainest of studs and wrist-links ... are all he ought to wear.

The Habits of Good Society (1859)

Gentlemen – Use no perfumes.

Etiquette for Ladies and Gentlemen (c.1870)

While freshness is essential to being well-dressed, it will be a consolation ... to reflect that a visible newness in one's clothes is as bad as patches and darns, and to remember that there have been celebrated dressers who would never put on a new coat till it had been worn two or three times by their valets.

The Habits of Good Society (1859)

To mention the important item of body linen:- never wear, if possible, a coloured shirt. Figures and stripes do not conceal impurity, nor should this be a desideratum with any decent man.

The Complete Etiquette for Gentlemen (c.1878)

Change your linen when at all dirty. This is the best guide ... if we have a cold, to say nothing of the possible but not probable case of tear-shedding on the departure of friends, or of a sensitive young lady over a Crimean engagement, we shall want more than one pocket-handkerchief per day.

The Habits of Good Society (1859)

Brummell made his reputation by the knot of his cravat, and even in so tiny a trifle a man may show his taste or want of it.

The Habits of Good Society (1859)

Trouser presses are no good; they are a snare and a delusion. They squeeze the life out of the exuberant and expressive trouser and leave it in a condition of impotence. Really good wool is actually alive; it must never be crushed to death. The best way to show a regard for trousers is to hang them in your wardrobe end upwards with hangers, and give them freedom to recover naturally from their exciting day.

Etiquette for Gentlemen ANON. (1925)

Appear at the breakfast-table in some perfectly pure and delicate attire — fresh, cool, and delicious, like a newly plucked flower.

Don't: A Manual of Mistakes and Improprieties
CENSOR (c.1880)

You may dress rather gaily for a drive.

Etiquette for Ladies and Gentlemen (c.1870)

CHAPTER IV

Manners for Dancing

Balls, Subscription Dances, Parties and Other Entertainments

DANCING

MISS MOLLIE COWPER

REPRESENTATIVE OF

MISS BELLE HARDING

(OF LONDON)

GIVES PRIVATE LESSONS AND HOLDS CLASSES

AT THE

HOTEL D'ANGLETERRE, SAINT-JEAN-DE-LUZ

AND AT BIARRITZ, AT THE HÉLIANTHE

ALL LATEST MODERN DANCES   CHILDREN'S CLASSES

APPLY, HOTEL D'ANGLETERRE, ST-JEAN-DE-LUZ

WITH THE THREE MOST dangerous areas of combat temporarily subdued and the invitation cards beginning to make an impressive line along the mantel-shelf, our would-be upper-crusty can begin to enjoy themselves. An invitation to move and mingle on happy, dressy occasions, obviously so more relaxed than the constraints of a watchful dinner or intense 'At Home', was just the ticket desired to form a 'better way of life'. A ball was the premier evening entertainment for all well-to-do young; music and dancing being recognized heralds of love, the glittering pastures where Cupid practised his arrows.

For certain, the captured prizes were worth their weight in gold ... as the delightful, anonymous 'Man in the Club Window' who with 'A Matron' was co-author of *The Habits of Good Society*, 1859 tells us:

> Balls are the paradise of daughters, the purgatory of chaperons, and the Pandemonium of Paterfamilias. But when he has Arabella's ball-dresses to pay for; when mamma tells him he cannot have the brougham to-night, because of Lady Fantile's dance; when he finds the house suddenly filled with an army of upholsterer's men, the passage barricaded with cane-bottomed benches, the drawing-room pillaged of its carpet and furniture, and in course of time himself bodily turned out of his own library with no more apology than, 'We want it for the tea to-night'; when, if he goes to bed, there is that blessed — oh! yes, blessed! — horn going on one note all night long, and, if he stops up, he has no room to take refuge in, and must by force of circumstances appear in the ball-room among people of whom he does not know one quarter, and who will perhaps kindly put the final stroke to his misery by mistaking him for his own butler; when Paterfam undergoes this and more, he has no right to complain, and call it all a waste of time and pure folly. Will he call it so when Arabella announces that she is engaged to the young and wealthy Sir Thysse Thatte, Bart., and that it was at one ball he met her, at another he flirted, at a third he courted, and at a fourth offered?
>
> Will he call it so when he learns that it is balls and parties — innocent amusements — which have kept his son Augustus from the gaming-table, and Adolphus from curacao?
>
> There is not half enough innocent amusement in England, and, therefore, there is far too much vice.

PERHAPS A FEW of those mid-nineteenth century sentiments still have echoes reaching to the present day?

Balls are given in town and country by society at large and these invitation balls include Hunt Balls, Military and Naval Balls, Bachelors' Balls, etc.

The Manners and Rules of Good Society (1912)

A ball begins between 10 and 11 ... There must be a cloakroom attendant, a man to call cabs and cars, a man to take charge of the door, a man to announce guests, a refreshment-buffet, ... and, at about 11-30 a sit-down supper.

The Book of Etiquette LADY TROUBRIDGE (1926)

A Hostess should receive her Guests at the head of the staircase at a ball in town, and at the door of the ball-room at a country house. She should shake hands with each ... in the order of their arrival.

Manners and Rules of Good Society (1912)

Any number over one hundred constitutes a 'large ball', and under fifty 'a dance'.

The Habits of Good Society (1859)

For the comfort of such chaperons as are present, a warm sitting-room should be available, and it may add to their pleasure if Bridge tables are arranged.

The Book of Etiquette LADY TROUBRIDGE (1926)

Large blocks of ice are frequently placed in convenient spots for the purpose of cooling the atmosphere.

The Manners and Rules of Good Society (1912)

The requisites for an agreeable ball are good ventilation, good arrangement, a good floor, good music, a good supper, and good company.

The Habits of Good Society (1859)

Feed the band well.

The Book of Etiquette LADY TROUBRIDGE (1926)

At a dance a piano band is frequently engaged, while at a ball a full band is requisite.

Manners and Rules of Good Society (1912)

Four musicians are enough for a private ball. If the room is not large, do away with the horn; the flageolet is less noisy, and marks the time quite well.

The Habits of Good Society (1859)

As regards ball dresses, there is perhaps only one rule that may be safely laid down. That is that the young lady coming out at her first ball invariably wears white.

Cassell's Book of Etiquette (1921)

As guests arrive, they are ushered into the cloak-rooms. A maid should be ... in that reserved for ladies, to give her aid in straightening dresses, arranging hair, and removing all trace of the slight disorder caused by the drive.

Cassell's Book of Etiquette (1921)

Draw on your gloves in the dressing-room, and do not be for one moment with them off in the dancing-rooms.

How to be a Lady W. NICHOLSON (c.1880)

You will see the dear debutantes holding up their skirts with a small ribbon loop attached to the end of the train, and, although I am told that this gruesome sight may now be seen at balls in 'London Society', I have up to now been spared.

The Social Fetich LADY GROVE (1907)

For large balls, you should have printed a number of double cards, containing on one side a list of dances; on the other, blank spaces to be filled up by the names of partners. A small pencil should be attached to each card, which should be given to each guest in the cloak-room.

The Habits of Good Society (c.1859)

Do not wear black or coloured gloves, lest your partner look sulky; even should you be in mourning, wear white gloves, not black. People in deep mourning have no business in a ballroom at all.

Hints on Etiquette (1836)

The unmentionable but most necessary disguise of the 'human form divine' is one that never varies in this country, and therefore I must lay down the rule: For all evening wear — black cloth trousers ... and tail-coat ... and waistcoat, stiff tight and comfortless. The plainer the manner in which you wear your misery, the better.

The Habits of Good Society (1859)

The neck-tie. For dinner, the opera, and balls, this must be white, and the smaller the better. The shirt-front ... plain, with unpretending small plaits.

The Habits of Good Society (1859)

A gentleman intending to dance should remove his sword, otherwise he should not do so.

Manners and Rules of Good Society (1912)

Cavalry officers should never wear spurs in a ball-room.

Mixing in Society THE COUNTESS OF ———— (1869)

If you are dancing merely for dancing's sake ... ask some of the wall-flowers or neglected ladies ... and very likely you will find the plain girls quite as agreeable companions as the pretty ones, and not so exacting.

Everybody's Book of Correct Conduct (1893)

Never hazard taking part in a quadrille, unless you know how to dance tolerably; for if you are a novice, or but a little skilled you will bring disorder into the midst of pleasure.

The Manners and Rules of Good Society (1912)

In waltzing, ladies should exercise great discretion in the acceptance of a partner. Those mazy circles, those pleasing gyrations, those soft loving attitudes must not be assumed with a stranger. Caution must be observed in this, and all similar circumstances.

A Manual of Etiquette for Ladies (1855)

It is not the correct thing for the lady to refuse the invitation of one gentleman, and then accept that of another for the same dance. Duels have been fought for smaller matters than this.

The Correct Thing in Good Society
FLORENCE HOWE HALL (1902)

We shall be assured that to spread the right hand with fingers well extended, in the middle of a lady's back, is the only correct way to hold your partner.

The Social Fetich LADY GROVE (1907)

Dance quietly; do not kick and caper about …: dance only from the hips downwards; and lead the lady as lightly as you would tread a measure with a spirit of gossamer.

Hints on Etiquette (1836)

We must avoid the awkwardness of a gallant sea-captain who, wearing no gloves at a dance, excused himself to his partner by saying, 'Never mind, Miss, I can wash my hands when I've done'.

The Habits of Good Society (1859)

A lady should not drink much wine and never more than one glass of champagne.

How to be a Lady W. NICHOLSON (c.1880)

Ball-room introductions cease with the object, viz., dancing; nor subsequently anywhere else can a gentleman approach the lady by salutation, or any other mode, without a re-introduction of a formal character.

How to be a Lady W. NICHOLSON (c.1880)

Flirting is always vulgar, but it is perhaps less dangerous in a ball-room than out of one; still, very well-bred girls will not … linger too long away from their chaperone. Four dances are quite as much as a young lady should give the same partner.

Etiquette for Ladies and Gentlemen (c.1870)

No man of taste ever makes an offer after supper, and certainly nine-tenths of those who have done so have regretted it at breakfast the next morning.

The Habits of Good Society (1859)

Subscription dances are sometimes invitation dances and sometimes not. Tickets for these dances are charged for singly or by the series ... During the winter months they are a feature in certain sets.

Manners and Rules of Good Society (1912)

Hunt balls are given for the benefit of a particular Hunt, and the tickets are bought as for any other subscription dance. Men members of the Hunt wear pink-evening coats. Men members of other Hunts ... wear the lapels of their evening-coats covered with silk of their own Hunt colour.

The Book of Etiquette LADY TROUBRIDGE (1926)

Theatre Parties: This is a favourite way of returning hospitality with many bachelors. It would not be considerate or tactful to take a party of people whose tastes inclined towards serious drama to a revue, or vice versa.

The Book of Etiquette LADY TROUBRIDGE (1926)

Charades: They are a great help in entertaining a room full of promiscuous people. No special talent is needed.

Cassell's Book of Etiquette (1921)

CHAPTER V

Manners for Sport

*Riding, Walking, Bicycling, Boating and Other
Dangerous Pastimes*

Art - Goût - Beauté

IN THE SIXTEENTH century the stamp of a 'compleat' gentleman was that he could swear a new oath every sentence, take tobacco and find it virtuous, run a friend or foe through with 'a bodkin' and write silly verses to a would-be mistress. By the eighteenth century these had been relegated to three new ones — the way he took snuff (opening the box with one hand was the secret), the ease with which he cut an old acquaintance, and the grace with which he bowed to a new one. Charismatic aristocrats then thought up another set — if a man could ride, fence and dance well, he was skilled enough for good society. Fencing, fortunately, had became a pursuit rather than a life-preserver by the 1800s (there could be no freedom in conversation when, instead of politely differing with you, a man's hand moved to his sword-hilt), but, for both sexes, the other two continued to underpin upper-class culture — and of this brace, riding was counted the nobler skill.

Thus, if our intrepid students of polite society are afeared of horses, they had better turn back now or heed some serious advice:

> About hunting I shall say little, because I know little, which is a confession you will find the wisest plan to make in the country. I shall only advise you not to hunt unless you have a good seat and a good horse, and never accept the loan of a friend's horse, still less an enemy's, unless you can ride very well. A man may forgive you for breaking his daughter's heart, but never for breaking his hunter's neck.
>
> *The Habits of Good Society* (1859)

It will be noted that a hunting-coat, which is in reality red, is always spoken of as pink, and that hounds are not referred to as dogs.

The Book of Etiquette LADY TROUBRIDGE (1926)

A lady who has a secure seat is never prettier than when in the saddle, and she who cannot make her conquests there, may despair of the power of her charms elsewhere.

The Manners that Win ANON. (1880)

A lady should be careful to sit straight in the middle of the saddle, with her face full towards the horse's head. Whatever the motion of the animal, you should attempt to cling as closely as possible to the saddle.

The Habits of Good Society (1859)

The woman's right hand is the whip hand; the left is the bridle hand. The near side of the horse is the left side, the side on which a woman rides, and which everyone mounts.

Etiquette for Ladies (1900)

Many ladies on horseback wear silk drawers.

The World of Fashion (1828)

The riding habit must be absolutely plain and free from ornament, usually dark in colour, of woollen stuff, and close fitting to the figure; the gloves should be strong leather, coming up well upon the wrist; the whip light and plain.

Etiquette for Ladies (1900)

You must avoid too fine a dress, such as patent leather boots, and should wear a cut-away in preference to a frock-coat. ... if we dress with scrupulous accuracy, we are liable to be subjected to a comparison between our clothes and our skill. A man who wears a red coat to hunt in, should be able to hunt, and not sneak through gates or dodge over gaps.

The Habits of Good Society (1859)

In mounting a lady on horseback the gentleman takes her left foot in his right hand, and when she springs he helps her in this manner to reach the saddle, afterwards adjusting her left foot in the stirrup and arranging her habit for her.

Manners for Men MRS HUMPHRY (1897)

When a man rides with a woman he would naturally take the left or near side, as better able to protect ... and converse with her, but as his horse may rub against her, or splash her dress, it is customary for him to ride on the off side.

Etiquette for Ladies (1900)

As regards riding in town, the hours for practice in the Row are from 8 to 10 a.m. in summer and 9 to 11a.m. in winter, for inexperienced riders; young ladies ride with a riding-master ... or a relative, as may be the case.

Manners and Rules of Good Society (1912)

A lady should never ride alone, except in quiet parts of the country. In London she would be taken for a demoiselle du cirque.

The Habits of Good Society (1859)

It is not etiquette for a young lady to ride out alone, with only a groom in attendance; and mothers who permit the violation of this rule or propriety are greatly to blame. We should not have so many disgraceful stories of young ladies running away with and marrying grooms or riding masters, if they were not improperly left to such low riding associates.

Etiquette for Ladies and Gentlemen (c.1870)

When Shooting or Fishing: Headgear is important ... Elaborate fly-away hats which will not remain on the head are impossible for sports and hard walking, and the woman inexperienced in country fashions should note that, when shooting and fishing, clothes of a colour which blend with the landscape are a necessity, or she will act as a danger signal for all the fish, flesh, and fowl in the neighbourhood.

The Book of Etiquette LADY TROUBRIDGE (1926)

Of late years a good many ladies, including some members of the Royal House, have gone in rather keenly for salmon fishing, ... A kilt skirt of rough tweed unhemmed, over a pair of tweed knickerbockers to match, a Norfolk jacket with plenty of pockets, ribbed woollen stockings, stout low-heeled shoes, and a deerstalker cap, form the most workmanlike costume for a woman to go fishing in.

Cassell's Book of Etiquette (1921)

In walking the feet should be moderately turned out, the steps should be equal, firm, and light. A lady may be known by her walk.

The Habits of Good Society (1859)

Two or three hours of the afternoon should be given to vigorous out-of-door exercise, to a long country walk, if not tennis, cricket, &c.

Home Education: A Course of Lectures to Ladies
CHARLOTTE M. MASON (1899)

Everybody should be in the open air for at least two hours daily; and if in ordinary health should walk at least four to six miles — not a dull rigid walk, but a brisk, joyous, exhilarating walk. It might be considered vulgar to perspire; but certainly you should adopt a degree of speed sufficient to bring a moisture on the skin and a glow to the cheek.

The Glass of Fashion
THE LOUNGER IN SOCIETY (1881)

A light cane may be carried, ... An umbrella is, as a rule, preferable.

Etiquette for Ladies and Gentlemen (c.1870)

To revert ... to the cane or walking stick. There is much to be deduced from the manner in which it is carried. The correct style is to hold it at an angle of forty-five degrees, with the ferule upper-most and forward.

Manners for Men MRS HUMPHRY (1897)

The fashionable hours for walking in the Park on Sundays are from 1 to 2p.m., both winter and summer; and from 5 to 7p.m. in the summer months.

Manners and Rules of Good Society (1912)

If you are walking with a woman in the country, — ascending a mountain or strolling by the bank of a river, — and your companion, being fatigued, should choose to sit upon the ground, on no account allow yourself to do the same, but remain rigorously standing. To do otherwise would be flagrantly indecorous and she would probably resent it as the greatest insult.

Decorum ANON. (1877)

A lady should conquer a habit of breathing hard, or coming in very hot, or even looking very blue and shivery.

The Habits of Good Society (1859)

Croquet is a very good test of cheerfulness under adversity ... there is perhaps no game in which a fairly good player can be quite as merciless towards an indifferent opponent.

Cassell's Book of Etiquette (1921)

The sudden spring into fashion of Battersea Park is entirely due to the rage for bicycling that has seized the ladies at the present moment. For mounting ... men-friends are in much requisition for steadying the machine and keeping it from wobbling.

Chit Chat LADY B (1895)

Bicycling Costume: The usual tailor-made, cut considerably shorter in the skirt and arranged with due consideration of the exigencies of wheeling, constitutes the ordinary cycling dress, with a neatly cut coat and a hat not over-trimmed.

Manners for Women MRS HUMPHRY (1897)

As soon as a yacht is in harbour, and the ensign is flying at the stern, calls may be paid to those on board.

Etiquette for Women G.R.M. DEVEREUX (1919)

Never think of venturing out with ladies alone, unless you are perfectly conversant with the management of a boat ... Let the ladies be comfortably seated, and their dresses arranged before starting. Be careful you do not splash them, either by first putting the oar into the water or subsequently.

Etiquette for Ladies and Gentlemen (c.1870)

The usual [boating] costume for gentlemen is white flannel trousers, white rowing jersey, and a straw hat. Pea-jackets are worn when their owners are not absolutely employed in rowing.

Etiquette for Ladies and Gentlemen (c.1870)

Of late years ladies have taken ... to rowing. In moderation it is capital exercise for ladies ... They should wear a skirt barely touching the ground; they should also assume flannel Garibaldi shirts and sailors' hats ... We should observe, however, that it is impossible for any lady to row with comfort or grace if she laces tightly.

Etiquette for Ladies and Gentlemen (c.1870)

After a period of some indifference lawn-tennis has come to widespread favour. The modern player recognizes a good deal of etiquette as to the share of work expected in the mixed doubles, and women should understand this as regards joining with men who want to enjoy a scientific game.

Cassell's Book of Etiquette (1921)

A man, ... whether he aspires to be a gentleman or not, should learn to box. There are but few rules ... Strike out, strike straight, strike sudden. Two gentlemen never fight; the art of boxing is brought into use in punishing a stronger and more impudent fellow of a class beneath your own.

The Habits of Good Society (1859)

The skilled and accomplished skater usually keeps special boots for the purpose with the skates permanently affixed to them, thus avoiding that call on the good will of a friend to assist in fastening them.

Cassell's Book of Etiquette (1921)

Evening Bridge Parties are a formal, serious matter. The best players make a slip sometimes, and a nervous, less skilled exponent of the game may suffer intolerably under nagging, spiteful, angry or sarcastic remarks; even a bad or stupid partner or the most unpropitious cards are no excuse for loss of good temper and want of courtesy.

Etiquette Up To Date
CONSTANCE BURLEIGH (1925)

Many girls have obviously spoilt their chances of matrimony through Bridge playing.

Is Bridge Immoral? MRS ERIC PRITCHARD (1904)

CHAPTER VI

Manners for Sweethearts

Spinsters, Bachelors, Flatterers, Fast Girls and Other Charmers

HERE WE MEET the reality of the human condition and come to the nub of polite social contrivance. It was a way of finding a suitable mate. The rules of etiquette aided and abetted a self-imposed selection process. It was an amusing game, played in deadly earnest. Players, trusting the system, risked much to attract Mr or Miss Right from an equal social background, or, if the Fates smiled, even higher status. This was the unrevealed truth, the sole purpose behind so many of those engraved cards, kind calls, felicitous visits, and delightful invitations to exhausting 'At Homes', tiring receptions, tedious dinners and interminable balls.

The farmer wanted a wife, the lord wanted a lady. Daughters needed husbands — if possible, before the age of five and twenty.

Therefore, wise papas (and even wiser mammas), having concentrated many hours of many years on discreet promotion, reconnoitring numerous difficulties (namely, other parents) to lure prospective suitors for their daughters (or their sons), watched and waited for a happy outcome. Often as not, they had also paid out large amounts of money in this venture — and earnestly hoped and prayed for a goodly return on investment.

As our Man in the Club-Window says:

> The Bachelor: What a happy man! He is as much courted as a voter at an election; he is for ever being bribed by mammas and feasted by papas; nothing is complete without him; he is the wit at dinner, the 'life' at the tea-fight, an absolute necessity in the ball-room, a

sine qua non at fete and pic-nic, and welcome everywhere. Indeed, I don't know what society can do without him.

Happier still is the young lady, for whom so many allowances are made. To her the ball is a real delight, and the evening party much more amusing than to any one else. If she lacks beauty, she will not succeed without conversational powers; and if she has beauty, she will soon find that wit is a powerful rival. With the two she can do what she will; all men are her slaves.

The Habits of Good Society (1859)

If you would have a serene old age never woo a girl who keeps a diary.

The Cynics Rules of Conduct
CHESTER FIELD JR. (1906)

Never encourage the suit of a man upon whom you have no intention of bestowing your hand.

A Manual of Etiquette for Ladies (1855)

A first attraction of a very young man is likely to be a lady of mature years, and ... when it can be indulged without ridicule or scandal, and has for its object a woman of taste and character, is a great good fortune. It is the true and natural mode of completing the education. Such a woman is just the teacher and friend a young man needs to polish his manners, refine his taste — and ripen his heart.

The Complete Etiquette for Gentlemen (c.1878)

There is one subject which a young lady should always keep secret in her own bosom, nor reveal it to her dearest friend, that is when she first becomes aware of love's pleasing emotions without being certain that her attachment is even returned.

How to be a Lady W. NICHOLSON (c.1880)

Courtship is often ... a series of deceptions. Both persons show their best and most amiable qualities, not intentionally, but because they cannot help it. There is a mutual hallucination; a haze of passion which heightens every charm and conceals every defect. It is difficult, therefore, for them to exercise that amount of prudence ... which others advise. But they can always avoid committing a breach of etiquette.

The Complete Etiquette for Gentlemen (c.1878)

It is only in the very humblest ranks of courting couples that people ever walk arm-in-arm nowadays.

Cassell's Book of Etiquette (1921)

A public display of affection anywhere and at any time is unrefined. Love is sacred, and its expressions should not be exposed to the rude comments of strangers.

The Book of Etiquette LADY TROUBRIDGE (1926)

There are few actions so atrociously familiar as a wink. I would rather kiss a lady outright than wink or leer at her.

The Habits of Good Society (1859)

A lady will offer her lips to be kissed only to a lover or a husband, and not to him in company.

How to be a Lady W. NICHOLSON (c.1880)

The custom of withdrawing the glove before shaking hands with a lady is now a thing of the past. It originated from the knight taking off his iron gauntlet, which would have hurt the hand of his 'faire ladye'. No longer do we see gentlemen carrying a creased glove, or wearing one untidily large, in order to avoid the awkwardness of keeping the lady waiting while he drags it off.

Cassell's Book of Etiquette (1921)

The French code is a good one: 'Give your hand to a gentleman to kiss, your cheek to a friend, but keep your lips for your lover.'

How to be a Lady W. NICHOLSON (c.1880)

It is now held by many that the prudent and modest maiden should not even allow her lover, (even after their engagement), to kiss her. Not until after marriage should such a favour be granted.

Modern Manners and Social Forms
JULIA M. BRADLEY (1889)

The gifts made by ladies to gentlemen are of the most refined nature possible: they should be little articles not purchased, but deriving a priceless value as being the offspring of their gentle skill; a little picture from their pencil or a trifle from their needle.

How to be a Lady W. NICHOLSON (c.1880)

The less your mind dwells upon lovers and matrimony, the more agreeable and profitable will be your intercourse with gentlemen.

A Manual of Etiquette for Ladies (1855)

To keep a lady's company six months is a public announcement of an engagement.

Search Lights on Health
PROF. B.G. JEFFERIS and J.L. NICHOLS (1896)

Don't be continually talking about what a great beau you were in your younger days. That you are still unmarried is sufficient evidence that you were, at least, an unsuccessful one.

Don'ts for Everybody
Compiled by FREDERIC REDDALE (1907)

With regard to flirtation, it is difficult to draw a limit where the predilection of the moment becomes the more tender and serious feeling, and flirtation sobers into a more honourable form of devoted attention.

The Habits of Good Society (1859)

Never read in company. A gentleman or lady may, however, look over a book of engravings with propriety.

Martine's Hand Book of Etiquette (1865)

Every woman is more or less influenced by flattery, like strong wine it is pleasant to swallow, and the emptiest heads are soonest affected by it. Be sure that the person who flatters you has always some sinister object in view.

How to be a Lady W. NICHOLSON (c.1880)

The fast girl is flattered, admired openly, but secretly condemned.

The Habits of Good Society (1859)

At a reception the chaperone promenades the room, speaking to her friends, and the young ladies must keep within her orbit, like satellites within the system of the planet. She will not be less cautious in supervising their choice of girl-friends than of male acquaintances; for a 'fast' girl, given to slang and chaff, and prone to familiarities with the men which, however innocent, are indecorous and painful, carries about with her an infectious atmosphere.

The Glass of Fashion
THE LOUNGER IN SOCIETY (1881)

Most women would rather have any of their good qualities slighted, than their beauty.

Martine's Hand Book of Etiquette (1865)

If you pay lady a compliment, let it drop from your lips as if it were the accidental and unconscious expression of a profound truth.

The Standard Book on Politeness, Good Behavior and Social Etiquette ANON. (1884)

If a gentleman gives you reason to believe that he wishes to engage your affections, seek the advice of your parents, that they may gain for you every necessary particular with regard to his morals and disposition, and means of suitably providing for you.

Martine's Hand Book of Etiquette (1865)

We shall make no attempt to prescribe a form for popping the question. Each must do it in his own way; but let it be clearly understood and admit no evasion. A single word — yes, less than that on the lady's part, will suffice to answer it.

How to be a Lady W. NICHOLSON (c.1880)

Matrimony should be considered as an incident in life, which, if it comes at all, must come without any contrivance of yours.

A Manual of Etiquette for Ladies (1855)

Remember that if a gentleman makes you an offer, you have no right to speak of it. If you possess either generosity or gratitude for offered affection, you will not betray a secret that does not belong to you.

Martine's Hand Book of Etiquette (1865)

Lovers would do well to remember that hedges have ears as well as stone walls.

Gems of Deportment ANON. (1880)

CHAPTER VII

Manners for Wedding

Betrothal, Presents, Bridal Array, The Marriage,
Breakfast, Broken Engagements and Other Mishaps

WE HAVE ARRIVED at the finest juncture in
Good Society; the arrangement of a marriage.
The rules of behaviour surrounding Holy
Wedlock were both enchanting and alarming, well-suiting

the emotions manifest in this deed. The man, having offered and been accepted, was, instantly, taken into the intimacy of his adopted relations.

> Could there be any thing more terrifying to a modest man, than what I experienced the night after my proposals had been accepted. It was at 'my intended's' parents, where a whole coterie of her friends, brothers, and sisters, had assembled to canvass over the length of my purse — the breadth of my merits — the most of my expectations — and in fact, the long and short of all I was worth in the world.
>
> Letter to the Editor, *The World of Fashion* (1828)

NOW, WITH TRIUMPH, the bride's mother embarked upon that grand campaign for which she had prayed; as one Victorian writer remarked, 'matrimony is with women the great business of life, whereas with men it is only an incident'. The betrothed couple were — sometimes — allowed to be alone in each other's company (possibly for the first time since they met) and would hurry about meeting and greeting opposing sets of relatives. It was for the gentleman's family to 'call' first; for him to present the first gift ... as a seal upon the affair. Absence of such a gift was thought to imply want of earnestness in the matter.

> This present generally consists of some personal ornament, say, a ring, and should be handsome, but not so handsome as that made for the wedding-day.
>
> *The Habits of Good Society* (1859)

The beginning of an engagement is usually marked by the gift of a ring from the man to his fiancee. Former superstition forbade that this should be set with emeralds or opals, — the former were held to denote jealousy and the latter ill-luck.

Cassell's Book of Etiquette (1921)

If she [the bride] has a fortune, she should, in all points left to her, be generous and confiding, at the same time prudent. Many a man may abound in excellent qualities, and yet be improvident. Upon every account, therefore, it is desirable for a young lady to have a settlement on her.

An allowance for dress should also be arranged; and be administered in such a way that a wife should not have to ask for it at inconvenient hours, and thus irritate her husband.

The Habits of Good Society (1859)

The invitations should be issued from three weeks to a fortnight before the wedding-day. The invitations should be issued in notes printed in ink; they are now seldom printed in silver.

Manners and Rules of Good Society (1912)

Announcement is also made of approaching weddings of any social importance in the three leading morning papers — namely *The Times*, the *Daily Telegraph*, and the *Morning Post*, which make a charge of a guinea each for the insertion.

Cassell's Book of Etiquette (1921)

Every one who is invited to a wedding invariably makes the bride or bridegroom a present; it is the received rule to do so. Many send presents before the invitations are sent out.

Manners and Rules of Good Society (1912)

To be sure, when you send a present, that the price is not marked on it; and never to send one with the carriage unpaid.

Everybody's Book of Correct Etiquette
M.C. (1893)

Banns must be published in the church of the parish in which the lady lives, and also that in which the gentleman resides, for three continuous Sundays prior to the marriage.

Cassell's Book of Etiquette (1921)

The Responsibilities of a Bridegroom from a pecuniary point of view commence from the moment of his engagement.

Manners and Rules of Good Society (1912)

It is the duty of the best man to see his friend is called in good time, pay the hotel bill, &c. He should then accompany the bridegroom to the church, taking care to be in good time. On arrival – the two gentlemen retire to the vestry, and at this time it is – for the bridegroom's man to give the clergyman his fee, also the clerk, pew-opener, beadle, bell-ringer, &c., as it saves confusion afterwards.

Etiquette for Ladies and Gentlemen (c.1870)

Favours are still given at large weddings ... Four young ladies (friends of the bride) are stationed in the [church] porch with great baskets of favours, and packets of large pins, which they offer to each guest on arrival.

Etiquette-Up-To-Date
LUCIE HEATON ARMSTRONG (c.1924)

It is the privilege of the best man to present the bride with her bouquet.

Etiquette for Ladies and Gentlemen (c.1870)

The Best Man should be a bachelor ... he should stand at his right hand during the ceremony — a little to the rear of the groom — and should render him the trifling service of handing him his hat at the close of it.

Manners and Rules of Society (1912)

The trousseau consists, in this country, of all the habiliments necessary for a lady's use in the first two or three years of her married life; like every other outfit there are always a number of articles introduced into it that are next to useless, and are only calculated for the vain-glory of the ostentatious.

The Habits of Good Society (1859)

The lingerie must be chosen with due regard for the wearer's future position in life, for garments so fragile that they need constant repair … are only for the rich.

The Book of Etiquette LADY TROUBRIDGE (1926)

The Bride's Trousseau should be marked with the initials of the name she is to take.

Manners and Rules of Good Society (1912)

The bridesmaids are from two to eight in number. It is ridiculous to have many, as the real intention of the bridesmaid is, that she should act as a witness of the marriage.

The Habits of Good Society (c.1859)

As to the wedding dress, the rule still obtains that the bride should wear white.

Cassell's Book of Etiquette (1921)

The bride's white satin is now often replaced by silk muslin, chiffon or lace. Should she elect to be married in travelling dress, her bridesmaids wear smart visiting costumes — A widow, when marrying again, wears grey, mauve heliotrope, lavender, biscuit or any tint not mournful.

Manners for Women MRS HUMPHRY (1897)

A newly-married man should wear a blue coat, with gilt buttons; a quilted under waistcoat, or one of white velvet; small-clothes of black kersey-mere; silk stockings, with open clocks; shoes and buckles; his shirt frilled and ruffled, with lace laid in plaits like those of cambric; a muslin cravat, tied in the English manner, with the ends floating, fastened by a large diamond pin.

The World of Fashion (1828)

The usual dress of a bridegroom consists of a very dark blue frock-coat, light trousers, light or white scarf-tie, patent boots, and a new hat.

Manners for Men MRS HUMPHRY (1897)

With reference to the choice of horses for the occasion, at one time a pair of greys were considered indispensable for the bride's carriage … But that is now all changed, and it is thought better taste to have browns or bays. The fact is that a smart pair of greys has been found to attract much notice, with the consequence that an undesirable crowd frequently assembles at the bride's house. This gathering is mainly composed of nurse-girls in charge of perambulators, butchers' boys … to say nothing of fishmongers' – , whose proximity is not always pleasant.

Manners for Women MRS HUMPHRY (1897)

The bridesmaid, where there is but one – rides in the same carriage with the bride; stands beside her during the ceremony, holding her glove while the ring is placed on her finger.

A Manual of Etiquette for Ladies (1855)

Nobody cries at a modern wedding, neither the bride nor her mother.

Etiquette-Up-To-Date
LUCIE HEATON ARMSTRONG (c.1924)

Tears are now bad form. The bride who cries at her wedding is considered to pay her bridegroom a very bad compliment.

Manners for Women MRS HUMPHRY (1897)

Upon the conclusion of the ceremony, it was the old-fashioned way, and natural enough … for the happy man to kiss his wife, even within the church, but it is not etiquette. Prince Albert did not kiss the queen; her majesty was, however, saluted by the Duke of Sussex.

A Manual of Etiquette for Ladies (1855)

When rice is thrown after a bride it should be scattered by the married and not by the unmarried ladies present.

Manner and Rules of Good Society (1912)

The newly-married pair must be the first to leave the church. They now proceed in one carriage. Sometimes they leave immediately for the country, but sometimes return for a short period, namely, to the wedding breakfast and then start for the honeymoon.

A Manual of Etiquette for Ladies (1855)

Strewing the Bride's Path with Flowers from the church

to the carriage by village children is a custom much followed at weddings which take place in the country.

Manners and Rules of Good Society (1912)

Those of the company who have not attended the service, or have had not opportunity of speaking to the newly-married couple, offer their congratulations on being shown to the drawing-room, where all assemble prior to the breakfast. Here ... are displayed the wedding presents, which vary in number and value, according to the position and popularity of the bride.

The Glass of Fashion
THE LOUNGER IN SOCIETY (1881)

The breakfast is arranged on one or more tables, and is generally provided by a confectioner when expense is not an object.

The Habits of Good Society (1859)

Wedding breakfasts nowadays ... are simpler functions than they were. Even among the aristocracy, reduction of incomes and the general rise in the cost of living have made themselves felt in various ways.

The Art of the Table
C. HERMANN SENN, MBE, FRHS (1923)

Speeches are out of fashion; it is the rarest thing in the world if some old friend of the family proposes the health of the bride.

Etiquette-Up-To-Date
LUCIE HEATON ARMSTRONG (c.1924)

All other toasts are optional, but it is de rigueur that the health of the clergyman or clergymen who tied the knot, if present, should be drunk.

The Habits of Good Society (1859)

We are a conservative people, and cling to the old traditions most firmly when they have least to recommend them: two white satin slippers, therefore, must be thrown after the bride, one by the best man, the other by the bridesmaid, as a sign that she [the bride] is dismissed from the ranks of the unmarried.

The Glass of Fashion
THE LOUNGER IN SOCIETY (1881)

The bridal wreath, the bouquet and the orange blossoms from the wedding-cake, if treasured as mementoes of the happy event, should be preserved in the recesses of a locked drawer, and not exhibited under glass shades in the drawing-room.

Manners and Rules of Good Society (1912)

The honeymoon is seldom protracted beyond ten days or a fortnight. On its conclusion, the bride reappears in society, and for three months, the first time she dines at any house she generally takes precedence, as a bride, of all the other ladies. For these dinners she usually wears her wedding-dress, but without the orange flowers.

The Glass of Fashion
THE LOUNGER IN SOCIETY (1881)

There is something about going to a wedding which leaves one very dull in the evening. An evening at the theatre is the pleasantest solution of the problem of finishing up this difficult day.

Etiquette-Up-To-Date
LUCIE HEATON ARMSTRONG (c.1924)

When an engagement is broken off, all letters and presents should be returned on both sides.

All wedding presents received by the bride-elect should likewise be returned to donors. The mother of the bride should announce to all whom it may concern, the fact that the engagement is at an end.

Manners and Rules of Good Society (1912)

When a man marries, it is understood that all former acquaintanceship ends.

Hints on Etiquette (1836)

To reveal details respecting a wife's personal charms to another man is past all excuse.

The Book of Culture HARRIET LANE (1922)

CHAPTER VIII

Manners for Travelling

Horse-drawn Carriage, Steam Railway, Sea Voyages, the
Motor-Car and Other Itinerant Information

RICH AND ARISTOCRATIC families had always travelled – originally compelled by courtly camp-following, it then developed into cumbersome domestic arrangements that required seasonal visits to either town or country. Thus, having seen all they wished to see of their own land, they became eager to go and look at everyone else's and thereby arranged the Grand Tour as a sort of educational sight-seeing for mature students.

Transport was never easy; in former centuries, the only way Lord North could get down to see Lady South, in comparative comfort, was via his horse-drawn carriage, but, come the 1890s, he could have popped down by steam rail – or motor-car. Thankfully, by then, sea voyages were no longer contemplated with dread – fretting at the thought of mutinous sailors and meagre rations (well, not on P & O, anyway), but were enjoyed as part of the smart agenda of social high life. Steaming in luxury on the ocean waves brought with it a new set of rules for polite behaviour that self-help authors were keen to explain. Travelling in style, including a section on opening and closing train windows, provided another chapter by the time King George V, who was a stickler for good manners, was crowned in 1911.

It is the correct thing to put one's affairs into satisfactory order before starting on a long journey.

Everybody's Book of Correct Conduct M.C. (1893)

It is not the correct thing to outrage the manners and customs of the country you are visiting. In Rome you should do as the Romans do; if you cannot manage this, do not visit them. They do not ask to be insulted by strangers.

Everybody's Book of Correct Conduct M.C. (1893)

It ought to be part of our patriotic feeling to endeavour to convey as agreeable an idea as possible of ourselves to those countries which we honour with our distinguished presence in our little trips.

Manners for Women MRS HUMPHRY (1897)

In driving with ladies, a man must take the back seat of the carriage, and when it stops, jump out first, and offer his hand to let them out.

The Habits of Good Society (1859)

Although ... young, his manners savour much of the old school; he never takes the wall of any woman; he never passes a carriage whilst the ladies are getting in or out – but his principal motive is to have the honour of handing them into the carriage; some ... so little used to that sort of politeness from a stranger, or from timidity ... decline his assistance.

The World of Fashion (1828)

Do not take a stiff-handled parasol, or a large umbrella, in your friend's carriage to scratch the paint.

Etiquette for Ladies and Gentlemen (c.1870)

In getting into a hansom, if you are the first to get in you should turn yourself dexterously into the corner nearest the step you mounted by, so that the companion who follows you may have the farther seat, and not have to screw himself around the door.

Etiquette for Women G.M.R. DEVEREUX (1919)

In your own carriage you should always give the front seat to a visitor, if you are a man, but a lady leaves the back seat for a gentleman.

The Habits of Good Society (1859)

In entering a train or omnibus a man assists the lady he is escorting. If there are a number of people entering — he prevents her being pushed or squeezed.

The Book of Etiquette LADY TROUBRIDGE (1926)

The sight of a seat kept by an umbrella or rug apparently fills certain perverse persons with a desire to take possession.

The Social Fetich LADY GROVE (1907)

In railway travelling you should not open a conversation with a lady unknown to you, until she makes some advance towards it. On the other hand, it is polite to speak to a gentleman. If you have a newspaper, and others have not, you should offer it to the person nearest to you. An acquaintance begun on a railway may sometimes go farther, but, as a general rule it terminates when one of the parties leaves the carriage.

The Habits of Good Society (1859)

Beware of yielding to the sudden impulse to spring from the carriage to recover your hat which has blown off, or a parcel dropped.

Dr. Lardner's Rules from 'Travelling Past and Present'
Edited by THOMAS A. CROAL (1877)

The person sitting nearest to the window and facing the engine, is supposed to have the control of the sash, and if any other occupant of the carriage should wish for any alteration of its position, it would be necessary to ask the permission of the other.

Good Manners MRS HUMPHRY (1902)

Spit in the spittoon and throw refuse out of the window.

Modern Manners and Social Forms
JULIA M. BRADLEY (1889)

It is excessively rude for anyone to reach across window-seat passengers to raise or lower the window without at least a polite question or apology. Sometimes a change of seats may be arranged to mutual advantage.

Etiquette Up To Date
CONSTANCE BURLEIGH (1925)

Ladies travelling alone — will thank gentlemen who raise or lower windows, coldly but politely.

Collier's Cyclopedia of Commercial and Social Information
Compiled by NUGENT ROBINSON (1882)

To crowd a railway-carriage up with ... bulging leather bags is far from considerate, and therefore becomes impolite.

Good Manners MRS HUMPHRY (1902)

Sea-sickness renders its victims very querulous, and few like to be continually reminded of their condition by inquiries too often repeated of – 'Do you feel any better?' or 'Do you think you could eat something?'

Etiquette for Ladies (1900)

A bed pan would also be useful, though this would be rather too large for the special medical case.

Hints on Outfit for Travellers in Tropical Countries
CHARLES FORBES HARFORD, MA (1911)

All immoral or indecent acts of conduct, improper liberties or familiarities with the female passengers, blasphemous, obscene, or indecent language, or language tending to a breach of the peace, swearing, gambling, drunkenness, fighting, disorderly, riotous, quarrelsome, or insubordinate conduct and also all deposits of filth or offensive acts of uncleanliness in the between decks, are strictly prohibited.

From the *Order in Council*, for promoting order and health in passenger *Ships* to any of Her Majesty's possessions abroad (7th January, 1864)

It is not usual for a woman to travel across the ocean alone.

Book of Etiquette, Vol. 2 LILIAN EICHLER (1921)

Unless travelling luxuriously or during a slack season, you will probably share a cabin with one or more other passengers and here the need for courtesy, tolerance and unselfishness is sure to arise.

Etiquette Up To Date
CONSTANCE BURLEIGH (1925)

To receive the attentions of strange gentlemen on board is only permissible to the extent of procuring you a camp stool.

Etiquette for Ladies (1900)

Women should dress quietly and inconspicuously when travelling. Anything startling should be avoided.

The Book of Etiquette LADY TROUBRIDGE (1926)

The cummerbund is a useful article of clothing, especially for men in the evening. It does away with the need for a waistcoat, which often proves hot and uncomfortable, and yet provides the necessary safeguard against chill to the abdominal organs.

Medical Hints
WILLIAM HENRY CROSSE, MD (c.1890)

Ladies should take their usual thin summer dresses, but shun openwork blouses, which are a source of great attraction to mosquitoes, and owing to the action of the sun, give the wearer the appearance of being tattooed when she appears in evening dress.

Aspinall's Pocket Guide to the West Indies (1907)

What every Woman Needs at Sea. A cane deck folding chair with leg rest, in which she can, if so desired, recline at full length. It should be distinctly marked with the owner's name in a prominent place.

A good supply of old underclothing, which can be thrown overboard when soiled.

An india-rubber hot water bottle. This will be found the greatest comfort in an attack of mal de mer.

Some amusing novels.

Hygeia A LADY DOCTOR (1895)

Although the rule of social etiquette touching formal introduction is relaxed on board ship to the extent of permitting passengers to talk to one another, ... it is, for instance, very bad form to use some one else's deck-chair.

The Book of Etiquette LADY TROUBRIDGE (1926)

Any lonely British woman, finding that she has been led into an undesirable position or difficulties from which she cannot extricate herself, should at once seek the advice from the British Consul.

Etiquette Up To Date
CONSTANCE BURLEIGH (1925)

Europeans are inclined to associate lack of social form and social restraint with moral laxity in women.

The Book of Culture HARRIET LANE (1922)

Travellers who are not fastidious as to their table-companions will often find an excellent cuisine, combined with moderate charges, at the hotels frequented by commercial travellers.

Handbooks for Travellers (Southern France)
BAEDECKER (1907)

The heat increases one's thirst by producing perspiration, and the only remedy to this is tea, for there is nothing so effectual in allaying thirst. It will often be found useful to carry a bottle of cold tea. Old travellers frequently carry in their holsters, instead of pistols, a small teapot, with a paper of tea, and another of sugar, on the one side, and a cup.

Turkey in Asia MURRAY (1878)

Ladies may visit the better-class cafes without dread at least during the day.

Handbooks for Travellers (Southern France)
BAEDECKER (1907)

A woman would not be admitted to an hotel without luggage, except under very exceptional circumstances, such as an accident.

The Book of Etiquette LADY TROUBRIDGE (1926)

Practically every one motors more or less nowadays, — it is the most convenient form of transport for long or short journeys, for shopping and paying calls or for a run in the Park during the fashionable afternoon driving hour in the London season.

Etiquette Up To Date
CONSTANCE BURLEIGH (1925)

When age, rank, or other reasons for precedence do not have to be considered amongst members of a motoring party, it is only courteous for those who have enjoyed the most coveted seats to change places on a return trip, with those who have been less favoured.

Etiquette Up To Date
CONSTANCE BURLEIGH (1925)

While there are several little repairs that it would be impossible to remedy if wearing gloves, the majority of work on a car (filling tanks, &c. &c.) can be done just as well if one's hands are protected by wash-leather gloves. You will find room for these gloves in the little drawer under the seat of the car.

This little drawer is the secret of the dainty motoriste. What you put in it depends upon your tastes, but the following articles are what I advise ... A pair of clean gloves, an extra handkerchief, clean veil, powder-puff, hair-pins and ordinary pins, a hand mirror – and some chocolates are very soothing.

The Woman and the Car
DOROTHY LEVITT (1909)

Older or delicate people should not be perched on a 'dickey seat'.

Etiquette Up To Date
CONSTANCE BURLEIGH (1925)

If you are going to drive alone in the highways and byways it might be advisable to carry a small revolver.

The Woman and the Car
DOROTHY LEVITT (1909)

CHAPTER IX

Manners for Letter-Writing

Invitation, Congratulation, Condolence, Proposals and Other Epistolary Advice

ONCE UPON A TIME, writing a letter had to be vital since the business of communicating on paper with someone at a distance — via the hazards of a messenger-on-horseback delivery — was unreliable, expensive and took forever (similar to now, actually). They needed to be pretty important words to make you desperate enough to pop them in the post. Mothers, however, have always worried about their sons:

> Good Ned,
>
> I have new received your letter ... I take it for a greate bllesing that your worthy tutor gives so good a testimony

of you ... Deare Ned, if you would have any thinge, send word: or if I thought a coold pye, or such a thinge, would be of any pleasure to you, I would send it. But your father says you care not for it, and Mrs P. tells me when her sonne was at Oxford, and shee sent him such thinges, he prayed her that shee would not ...

> Your most Affectinat mother
> tel death,
> Brilliana Harley

Letters of Lady Brilliana Harley (1638)

THE NINETEENTH CENTURY saw all types of correspondence become a minor art. Having instigated a national postal service, the Victorians were dedicated letter-writers, and none more so than the Queen. It was not called the Royal Mail for nothing. Daily, Her Majesty, besides entering thoughts and events in her diary, wrote letters to friends, distant family and close children — advice, approval or admonishings constantly flying from her neat pen. She could so easily have found success as an agony aunt. If ever there was a woman to whom the phrase 'Do keep in touch' guaranteed an immediate, polite response, it was that remarkable monarch.

Having before them such an exemplary correspondent, it would be foolish for our seeker of polite skills to neglect handwriting, the quality of notepaper, management of grammatical language and, last but not least, the placement of the stamp.

But before finally crossing the *t*'s or dotting the *i*'s it was wise to seek informed help. Beware, as one instructor puts it, 'The written word is inflexible; a verbal reproof is forgotten, but words written in anger — though the anger be but that of a moment — stand for all time.'

The letter of introduction, if actually given to its bearer, should be left open, that he may not incur the fate of the Persian messenger, who brought tablets of introduction recommending the new acquaintance to cut his head off.

The Habits of Good Society (1859)

When a letter asking a favour of a stranger requires a written reply, a stamp should be enclosed, a case in point being that of a request for a servant's reference.

Etiquette Up To Date
CONSTANCE BURLEIGH (1925)

There is no greater opportunity to show good taste — or bad — than in the type of notepaper we use. Anything startling in the way of stationary, — vivid colours, — address embossed in gold, very large crests of monograms, is in bad taste. The notepapers — are either white, cream, grey, or what in known as azure-tinted.

The Book of Etiquette LADY TROUBRIDGE (1926)

The use of the pencil (save for some unavoidable reason) in writing is as objectionable as the sending out of a letter with a blot.

The Book of Culture HARRIET LANE (1922)

In writing to persons decidedly your inferiors in station, avoid the probability of mortifying them, by sending mean, ill-looking notes.

Miss Leslie's Behaviour Book (1859)

Don't answer a royal invitation in the first person. Don't refuse it; nothing but death, or an infectious illness, being sufficient reason for doing so.

Etiquette for Women G.R.M. DEVEREUX (1919)

Envelopes should correspond in style and quality with the letter. Ruled paper, though admissible, is not such good style as unruled. Use good black ink; pale ink is inexcusable ... Blue ink is never safe to use for letters, for if it gets damp the writing will become illegible. Your letter should be folded with exact care to fit the envelope; the fewer the creases the better the letter will look when unfolded.

Complete Etiquette for Ladies (1900)

Very dainty young ladies affect a pink tinted paper and violet perfumed ink, upon which basis they begin a gushing correspondence with six or eight school friends, wherein the adjectives suffer much harm.

Gems of Deportment ANON. (1880)

Notepaper with a dainty flower in one corner is as much out of place in the writing desk of the middle aged as a flowery hat would be upon her head.

Manners for Girls MRS HUMPHRY (1901)

The correspondence card is an innovation of recent years, and is useful either for a short note enclosed in an envelope or employed as a post-card with a stamp of the right value affixed.

Cassell's Book of Etiquette (1921)

It used to be considered rather rude to conclude a letter on the first or second page. If our grandfathers or grandmothers did so, they almost invariably apologised for a brevity that in those days had the effect of curtness.

Manners for Women MRS HUMPHRY (1897)

Above all, never send a compliment or an inquiry in a post-script ... Nobody likes to see their name mentioned as an afterthought.

The Ladies' Book of Etiquette, and Manual of Politeness. FLORENCE HARTLEY (1873)

It is now considered in bad taste to write the letters 'P.S.' before anything which has to be added to a letter after it has been finished.

Etiquette Up To Date
CONSTANCE BURLEIGH (1925)

When sealing wax is required, either red or black (for mourning) is generally used; but we doubt if anyone could be found able to seal a letter neatly except a lady or gentleman of the olden school, so little occasion there is for the art to be practised.

Cassell's Book of Etiquette (1921)

A narrow border of black tells the story of loss as well as an inch of coal-black doom.

Manners and Social Usages
MRS JOHN SHERWOOD (1897)

Letters of condolence should be written as soon as one hears of the bereavement. Brevity without abruptness is the ideal in this case. Many people send their visiting cards — with a line of sympathy along the top ... It used to be the fashion to write letters of condolence on black-edged paper, just as a visit used to be paid in mourning, but both these ideas have gone out of date.

Etiquette-Up-To-Date
LUCIE HEATON ARMSTRONG (c.1924)

Widows of Peers. — If widows of Peers re-marry they lose their titles, save by courtesy, except in the case of the widow of an Honourable, who is never re-installed. The widow marrying again an inferior in rank assumes his rank.

Beeton's Complete Letter-Writer for Gentlemen
(c.1860)

Invitations should be sent to those in mourning the same as to other people, except during the first month of their bereavement ... The invitation will be declined of course, but it shows they are not forgotten. Do not blunder, however, and send an invitation to the dead.

Modern Manners and Social Forms
JULIA M. BRADLEY (1889)

If rude epistles be addressed to you put them in the fire and do not reply, unless they demand an apology. Then demand it politely and firmly, ignoring the offensive matter as much as possible.

Beeton's Complete Letter-Writer for Gentlemen
(c.1860)

Formally the style Esq. was only given to persons of acknowledged position, but it has become common to attach it to the name of everybody one is acquainted with.

Beeton's Complete Letter-Writer for Gentlemen
(c.1860)

Address strangers and those you wish to treat with formal respect as 'Sir' or 'Madam'. Formal letters conclude, 'I am, sir, your obedient servant' or 'I have the honour to remain, sir, your obedient servant.'

Only servants and small tradesmen subscribe themselves, 'Yours respectfully'.

Etiquette for Ladies and Gentlemen (c.1870)

Use as few parentheses as possible; it is a clumsy way of disposing of a sentence, and often embarrasses the reader.

The Lady's Guide to Complete Etiquette
EMILY THORNWELL (1886)

A Proposal: If the carefully studied phrases which you have repeated so many times and so fluently to yourself, will persist in sticking in your throat and choking you, put them correctly and neatly upon a sheet of the finest white note paper, enclose it in a fine but plain white envelope, seal it handsomely with wax, address and direct it carefully, and find some way to convey it to her hand.

How to be a Lady W. NICHOLSON (c.1880)

Many persons prefer, when communicating with entire strangers or correspondents with whom they wish to maintain entirely formal relations, to adopt the third person, thus:

The Croft,
Moorlands,
Jan. 4th, 1898.

Mrs Armitage-Browne has to thank Mrs King for her communication, but regrets that she does not see her way to allow her daughter to take any part in the theatrical performance referred to. She therefore returns, with her thanks and compliments, the papers which Mrs King has been good enough to send.

What Shall I Say? A Guide to Letter Writing for Ladies MRS HUMPHRY (1898)

Divorced Ladies lose all titles. They assume their maiden name, and Mrs. prefixed.

Beeton's Complete Letter-Writer for Gentlemen
(c.1860)

When the stamp is in the center at the top it signifies an affirmative answer to the question ... and when it is at the bottom, it is a negative. Should the stamp be on the right-hand corner, at an angle, it asks the question if the receiver of the letter loves the sender; while in the left-hand corner means that the writer hates the other.

The Century Book of Facts. Edited by
HENRY W. RUOFF (1908)

Public Bodies are addressed through their Secretaries.

Beeton's Complete Letter-Writer for Gentlemen
(c.1860)

CHAPTER X

Manners for Domesticity

*Guests, Hospitality, Servants (including Gratuities),
Carving, Conversation, and Other Doubtful Pleasures*

ONE OF THE IRKSOME duties of being a
member of Good Society was hosting the
number of guests who came to stay. Although
they never said it, the upper-classes took it for granted

they were always welcome — in your house. Likely this was true — and just as well — for it was generally accepted that visits, particularly to the country, would involve bed and board for as long as ... ? This was a tender area: one writer speaks of a visit that was made in 'old times', when travel was fatiguingly slow, by a young woman intending to stay with friends for a fortnight and making it last a further thirty years until she died. Another strain of welcoming the Society weekender — or longer lingerer — was that it might involve not just them but their staff, too.

> 17 June 1293 ... There came to dinner John of Brabant, with 30 horses and 24 valets at wages, and the two sons of Lord Edmund, with 30 horses and 21 valets, and they stay at our expense in all things, in hay, oats and wages.
>
> *Household Accounts of John of Brabant*

THE DILIGENT HOSTESS, like a wise virgin, kept her guest room or rooms in constant readiness, especially before the invention of the telephone, just 'in case' a letter, warning of an intended visit, should fail to arrive before the guest.

> When visits are attempted as 'agreeable surprises', they are seldom very agreeable to the surprised.
>
> *Complete Etiquette for Ladies* (1900)

When the London season is at an end ... The opportunity — seems to have come for a circle of visits to our country friends. We must begin by fixing the various stages of our journey: that is, if possible, in such wise that we can go from one to the other without crossing the same ground, and without leaving between any of them a gap of unoccupied time.

The Glass of Fashion
THE LOUNGER IN SOCIETY (1881)

A woman is said to have the entree of her friend's house when she is allowed or assumes the privilege of entering it familiarly at all times, and without any previous invitation — a privilege often abused.

Complete Etiquette for Ladies (1900)

In visiting a friend for a short stay never take a trunk so big that it suggests the possibility of an indefinite lingering.

Good Manners for All Occasions
MARGARET E. SANGSTER (1921)

It is to be supposed that ... the hostess has inspected the chamber of her guest, to see that none of the articles that are in all modern and well-furnished houses are wanting — two ewers of fresh water on the stand and three towels on the rail (two fine and one coarse), a footbath, and other requisites.

Complete Etiquette for Ladies (1900)

If a gentleman cannot dispense with his valet, or a lady with her maid, they should write to ask leave to bring a servant ... Children and horses are still more troublesome, and should never be taken without special mention made of them.

The Habits of Good Society (1859)

The boxes, which ought to be taken up at once to the bedroom, should be unstrapped and unlocked by the housemaid. Ladies who have maids pay no further heed, of course, to their belongings.

Etiquette for Women G.R.M. DEVEREUX (1919)

It is a poor compliment to your hostess to be shabbily dressed if she moves amongst well-dressed people, but it is equally embarrassing for her if she lives very unpretentiously and a guest arrives with – elaborate evening gowns, evidently expecting to have a very gay time, when only the simplest style of entertainment can be offered.

Etiquette Up To Date
CONSTANCE BURLEIGH (1925)

Titles may be as worthless as republicans and moralists declare them to be; but while they are socially and legally recognised, only a fool or a bore will attempt to ignore them. On the other hand, ... it is a singular vulgarity to be constantly dragging them into conversation – rolling them on the tongue, – as if such delicious morsels must not be too quickly got rid of. They 'my lord' a man as if the repetition of the magic syllables communicated to themselves a direct personal qualification, while 'your Grace' lifts them up into the seventh heaven of flunkeyism.

The Glass of Fashion
THE LOUNGER IN SOCIETY (1881)

To relieve the Hostess: Guests should manage to amuse themselves to some extent, and to leave the hostess free in the mornings to attend to her own private duties and household affairs. Try to be always punctual at meals; the work of both hostess and servants is considerably lightened if guests show such consideration.

Etiquette for Women G.R.M. DEVEREUX (1919)

The main point in a country house visit is to give as little trouble as possible.

The Habits of Good Society (1859)

Your servants should be well trained and instructed, and should obey every order given by the butler. A master or mistress should never speak to them at dinner, and they must be themselves as silent as trappists. They should wear light shoes that cannot creak, and if they have a napkin instead of gloves, you must see that their hands are perfectly clean.

The Habits of Good Society (1859)

Servants should wait at table in clean white gloves: there are few things more disagreeable than the thumb of a clumsy waiter in your plate.

Hints of Etiquette (1836)

Housemaid – Call ladies. Clean ladies' shoes and brush skirts. All housework not done by the other maids. Mend house linen and ladies' clothes. Tidy drawing-room while family are at luncheon, and again while dressing for dinner. Take charge of laundry. Wait at table if required.

Parlour and housemaids wear print in the morning, plain black, or dark uniform dresses if the employer provides them, in the afternoon, and caps and aprons with both.

The Book of Etiquette LADY TROUBRIDGE (1926)

It is customary for visitors to settle their own laundry bills.

Complete Etiquette for Ladies (1900)

Between-maid — Lights kitchen fire; does door step and brasses, grates and — the rougher work. Does vegetables, sets and clears servants' meals, helps cook, and does house-parlourmaid's work when the latter is out.

The Book of Etiquette LADY TROUBRIDGE (1926)

The butler is the most important person in the house-hold. He should be an honest, sober, conscientious servant; for from him the footmen will take their cue, and as he must have the care of the wine and the plate, temptations to dishonesty are not lacking.

A butler wears throughout the day a black, evening tail-coat, black waistcoat, white shirt, black bow or long tie, and dark striped trousers. Before late dinner he changes to the regulation dress-suit and white tie. He is provided with baize or striped linen apron for pantry wear.

The Book of Etiquette LADY TROUBRIDGE (1926)

Man-servant – Does blacking boots and carries coals.
Cleans windows, cleans pantry. Does all table work,
hall-door and sitting-room bells, and attends to sitting
room fires and telephone. Calls and valets gentlemen.
Polishes dining-room table. Takes charge of billiard-
table. Carries luggage.

The Book of Etiquette LADY TROUBRIDGE (1926)

Gratuities to Servants. The only fee expected from
ladies after paying a visit of some days, is one to the
housemaid, which ranges from 5 shillings to 10 shillings.
Young ladies give even less when visiting by themselves,
2 shillings and 6 pence being considered sufficient.

The fees expected from gentlemen are; To the butler
or footman who valets them and to the coachman if he
drives them to and from the station or takes charge of
their horses, and to the housemaid. The fee to the
butler is from 10 shillings to £1, and for a short visit
from 3 shillings to 5 shillings.

Manners and Rules of Good Society (1912)

Carving should form an essential part of every man's
education, as nothing is more pathetic – to the onlooker
than to see a man utterly ignorant of the art hacking,
mangling, or otherwise mal-treating some joint or bird
he may have been suddenly called upon to dispense.

The Complete Etiquette for Gentlemen (c.1878)

Bad carving used to spoil three good things on the part
of the carver, good joints, good temper, and a good
digestion ... and to short men it was a positive
infliction, for I need scarcely say, that under no

circumstances whatever could a man be permitted to stand up to carve.

But because the carving of joints, game, &c., at a side-table, is a foreign custom lately introduced into this country, there are people still found patriotic enough to prefer carving at the dinner-table. 'I like the good old English custom,' says one; 'I like to see a host dispensing his hospitality himself'; and in the country, where some hosts prefer meat to manners, it is still retained.

The Habits of Good Society (1859)

As wine is a very common subject of discussion at table it is quite necessary that every gentleman should be able to converse, intelligently, upon the character and quality of various wines … It is very embarrassing to be called upon for an opinion and not be able to give one. Besides, ignorance on the history and quality of wines may impress gentlemen with the idea that you have not been much in good company.

The Complete Etiquette for Gentlemen (c.1878)

The evening amusements vary, depending chiefly on the tastes or talents of the hostess, her family, or those she has about her. In some houses music is considered the only amusement worth contemplating.

Etiquette for Women (1919)

It is the misfortune of musical people generally to be such enthusiasts, that, once beginning, they seldom know when to leave off.

Hints on Etiquette (1836)

Be ready also to quit the instrument after finishing: in some cases, when once seated, ladies seem to be glued to the piano.

The Habits of Good Society (c.1859)

It is difficult to give any advice about suitable topics for conversation, but it easy to tell what to avoid. No one should introduce the atmosphere of the sick-room into the salon; it is as bad as though one were to walk into a ball-room in a dressing-gown.

Etiquette-Up-To-Date
LUCIE HEATON ARMSTRONG (c.1924)

All our comfort depends on our servants, and I don't know why they should be tiring as a topic, but they are. Terrible boredom sets in when a lady visitor selects Mary Jane as her only theme.

Etiquette-Up-To-Date
LUCIE HEATON ARMSTRONG (c.1924)

To invariably commence a conversation by remarks of the weather shows a poverty of ideas that is truly pitiable.

Laws and By-Laws of American Society
S.A. FROST (1869)

Conversation should be as varied and as charming as a beautiful bouquet to which everyone who comes has brought a flower.

Etiquette-Up-To-Date
LUCIE HEATON ARMSTRONG (c.1924)

Do not out stay your welcome. It is better to leave the day before, rather than the day after.

The Glass of Fashion
THE LOUNGER IN SOCIETY (1881)

Never allow any person above the rank of a shopman to leave the room without your ringing the bell for the street door to be opened.

Hints on Etiquette (1836)

It is courteous, after having spent some days at a friend's, to write to the hostess from the next place you visit, announcing your safe arrival, and gracefully alluding to the pleasant sojourn you made under her hospitable roof.

The Glass of Fashion
THE LOUNGER IN SOCIETY (1881)

CHAPTER XI

Manners for Children

*Infants, Baptism, Bad Boys, Haughty Daughters, Little
Geniuses and Other Obnoxious Offspring*

H OWEVER MUCH AN upper-crusty might
actually dislike children they were a vital
adjunct to the laws laid down for a well-
ordered, society life. Heirs, progeny, sons. These were
words that held sombre meanings for the landed classes.
The begetting of babies, whether from beneath gooseberry
bushes or elsewhere, had to be dealt with — and then the

whole thing handed over to Nurse as soon as possible. No truck was to be had with children. Train them early, train them tough — as you might a horse or a dog — and best of all, leave it to someone else to do.

There was no room for namby-pamby, lower-class sentiments where minors were concerned. So, if our 'socially uncertain' couple were fond of 'kiddies' — they had better start advertising for a tough professional to make sure no 'spoiling' went on from the start:

> Lady-Nurse required immediately. One baby. Experienced, strong. Good needlewoman. Perambulator. Dust nurseries. Church of England. London. N.
>
> *The Lady* (1901)

> At one time it was considered quite the correct thing to clothe the door-knocker in white kid on the birth of a child.
>
> *Cassell's Book of Etiquette* (1921)

> Within a day or two of the birth of a child an announcement of it should be sent to one or two of the best papers.
>
> *Etiquette for Women* G.R.M. DEVEREUX (1919)

> Small cards, announcing the name of the baby and date of its birth, are often printed and tied with white bebe ribbon to the mother's [visiting] card, and posted round to friends and acquaintances.
>
> *Complete Etiquette for Ladies* (1900)

Some little gift may be left or sent to the baby by intimate friends, also some flowers for the mother, but only a few choice blooms rather than quantities of a mediocre kind.

Etiquette Up To Date
CONSTANCE BURLEIGH (1925)

Tipping the Nurse: The parents of the child, on the occasion of the christening, tip her with gold, so do the godparents. Visitors used always to be expected by the nurse to slide a half-sovereign or something substantial into her palm, when they first called to see the baby, or when the baby was brought down to be shown to them.

Etiquette for Women G.R.M. DEVEREUX (1919)

As a Rule Six Weeks are allowed to elapse between the birth of the child and the date of the christening.

Manners and Rules of Good Society (1912)

At a Christening Ceremony – the clergyman, the father and mother, the sponsors, the nurse and the baby, gather around the font. The child should have cloak and bonnet removed before the ceremony begins.

The principal godmother should take her place at the clergyman's left, and at the proper time the baby is given into her arms by the nurse, and she in turn places it in the clergyman's left arm. After he has baptized the baby he hands it back to the nurse.

Etiquette for Women G.R.M. DEVEREUX (1919)

Two godfathers and one godmother stand as sponsors for a boy, and one godfather and two godmothers for a girl.

Etiquette Up To Date
CONSTANCE BURLEIGH (1925)

The father accompanies the clergyman to the vestry after the service, in order to give particulars necessary for registration, and also to distribute the proper fees. Legally, none can be claimed for a baptism, but custom has established the practice. Sometimes the clergyman receives a banknote, sometimes one or two guineas, sometimes only silver, according to the means and position of the parents.

Cassell's Book of Etiquette (1921)

There are, too, several hangers on of the church who expect to be tipped also, for no other reason that they could give, beyond the fact that it is an occasion, and a custom.

Etiquette for Women G.R.M. DEVEREUX (1919)

Friends make a personal choice when giving christening presents; godmothers frequently present to a girl godchild a rare piece of lace or a trinket for use in later years.

Complete Etiquette for Ladies and Gentlemen (c.1920)

One has heard, too, of godfathers who have placed a substantial sum in the bank which is not touched before the majority is reached, and of others who have bought stocks and shares for the fortunate little personage.

Cassell's Book of Etiquette (1921)

A proud grandmother, or devoted auntie, possibly a god-parent, frequently presents a handsome robe, a cloak or a hood, for the little one. The list we give, may, therefore, in such articles be curtailed — but we leave it to the judgement of the mother to decide what she must provide herself:

Six shirts, four swathes, three pilches, two head flannels, one dozen diaper towels, three night and three day flannels, three night-gowns, three long-cloth slips, three monthly gowns, six bibs, one robe trimmed embroidery, one merino cloak embroidered.

Turkish towelling is now much used instead of linen diapers, and it is in many ways superior. Flannelette, too, is sometimes used, but of this we have had no personal experience.

The Young Mother ANON. (1895)

On no account should robes be prepared with short sleeves, they should like monthly gowns, have sleeves to the wrist. The exposure of the arms is a frequent cause of pneumonia and death.

The Young Mother ANON. (1895)

Do not feed a child too often or you may ruin his digestive powers for life. A child of seven months old should be fed every two hours during the day, and perhaps twice in the night. A good cry is not at all bad for a child, and to feed him whenever he cries may save a little trouble at the time, but is nothing less than a piece of cruelty towards him.

Mother SISTER RACHEL (1895)

Neither a child nor anyone else should be permitted to be in the glare of the sun without his hat. If he be allowed, he is likely to have a sun-stroke, which might either at once kill him or might make him an idiot for the remainder of his life, which latter would be the worse alternative of the two.

Woman as Wife and Mother
PYE HENRY CHAVASSE (1870)

Do not put a Heavy Straw Hat onto a child's head.

Gas Should Never be Used in the Nursery, the best light is that of oil lamps. These should be hung well out of reach of the child, so there is no danger of them being upset. In the night-nursery use candles and night-lights.

Baby should never be Instructed to Walk. It will be stronger, and learn to walk earlier, with a more free and exact carriage, and better developed chest, if allowed to creep about by itself.

Games to be Commended. For giving strength to the chest, trunk, and arms battledore and shuttlecock is unrivalled. Among other games to be encouraged (for girls as well as boys) are kite-flying, cricket, tennis, badminton, croquet, rowing, swimming, running, jumping, and playing with balls.

from *Mother* SISTER RACHEL (1895)

Here is a hint for poor mothers, which may be of use when they are obliged to send their little children alone to school or elsewhere: label them with their full name and address. This plan is one that should be always adopted when a child is being sent on a railway journey alone.

Certainly if all the numerous children who go astray on bank holidays alone were properly labelled, a great deal of trouble would be saved by the police, who, without further ado, would dispatch them by the quickest way to their homes.

MRS ALEC TWEEDIE
('Isobel' of *Home Notes*) (1896)

Who that has the care of a rollicking four-year-old boy has not witnessed his delight over his first pocket? How many times the chubby hand finds its way therein, and the number of observations emanating from the young man's brain upon the subject is beyond estimation.

Home Chat (1895)

Nurse's Fourteen Rules on Manners for Boys:

1. Hat lifted in saying 'Good-bye' or 'How do you do?'

2. Hat lifted when offering a seat in a train or omnibus, or in acknowledging a favour.

3. Keep step with anyone you walk with.

4. Always precede a lady up the stairs, and ask her if you may precede her in passing through a crowd or public place.

5. Hat off the moment you enter a street door and when you step into a private hall or office.

6. Let a lady pass first, always, unless she asks you to precede her.

7. In the drawing-room, stand till every lady in the room is seated, also older people.

8. Rise if a lady comes in after you are seated, and stand till she takes a seat.

9. Look people straight in the face when speaking or being spoken to.

10. Let ladies pass through a door first, standing aside for them.

11. In the dining-room take your seat after ladies and elders.

12. Never play with your knife, fork or spoon.

13. Do not take your napkin in a bunch in your hand.

14. Eat as fast or as slow as others, and finish the course when they do.

Mother SISTER RACHEL (1895)

Don'ts for Boys.

Don't ever call your mother the 'old woman'.

Don't be ashamed to wear patched clothes if it is necessary.

Don't forget to champion those weaker than yourself.

Don't think it manly to smoke cigarettes.

Home Chat (1895)

Let the first pocket serve as an object-lesson for using the handkerchief. Teach him to use it himself quietly and without attracting notice. Urge the necessity of keeping his little nose presentable at all times.

Mother ANON. (1895)

Don't leave children to their own devices near a lion's cage.

Good Manners for All Occasions
MARGARET E. SANGSTER (1921)

Peevish temper, cross and frowning faces, and uncomely looks have sometimes been cured in France by sending the child into an octagonal boudoir lined with looking-glasses, where, whichever way it turned, it would see the reflection of its own unpleasant features.

Good Behaviour ANON. (1876)

It is very important that a mother should train her boys properly, from their earliest years. She must teach them that it is right for them to wait upon ladies. There is no surer sign of a 'middle class' point of view than when men say that anything will do for women. In the upper classes the men may be bad in many outward ways, but they pay every mark of respect to the women of their family.

Etiquette-Up-To-Date
LUCIE HEATON ARMSTRONG (c.1924)

The happiness of a family very much depends on the conduct of the daughters.

How to be a Lady W. NICHOLSON (c.1880)

At each succeeding term the school programme should be carefully gone through, with a view to seeing if the lessons that follow consecutively may not be too trying, and, if so, arrangements should be made with the head of the school to spare the girl a long run of monotonous subjects.

A Word to Women MRS HUMPHRY (1898)

Be diligent in your studies. Remember that you are placed at school for your own benefit. It is for your own advantage that you are required to study.

How to be a Lady W. NICHOLSON (c.1880)

It does wonders for a girl to lie down for even half an hour a day.

A Word to Women MRS HUMPHRY (1898)

CHAPTER XII

Manners for Death

Mourning, Apparel, Widows, Weeds, Wills and Other Undertakings

IF THERE WAS ONE rite of passage that Good Society observed to the letter it was death. Nobody understood the niceties accompanying eternal rest better. From the moment the dying breathed their last — if not a little before — the awesome business that followed was put on full alert. The Victorians, especially, left nothing to chance. Every nuance was catered for. The whole panoply of death was mobilized. Everyone who had a part to play was expected to do it to perfection. Grandeur, drama and voracious propriety were the elements looked for in the solemnities surrounding bereavement of the beau-monde. Due reverence was paid to the woeful garb, the shuttered windows and laurelled door, and the close relatives withdrawing from bright haunts of society.

It went without saying that a splendid funeral was not only expected, but demanded. This was the high point. It was noted with thrilling respect the slow-moving, wreath-mounted cortege, the blind carriages, the jet, velvet-swathed and feathered horses, the suitably suffering faces of the hired mutes, holding their eerie black-draped wands, the ells of tragic bombazine and sad, puckering crape. Quiet approval included the trailing length and handsome width of the weepers, the muffled hooves, muffled bells and muffled tears.

It was an occasion to send the spirit soaring and give the neighbours something to talk about.

Whatever the deceased's short-comings had been in life, it mattered not — in death they were as saints.

At the last trump, graceful decorum was all.

The great Lord Chesterfield, who had been a ceaseless tyrant on behalf of polite behaviour, and worried his own son to an early grave because of it, is reported, on receiving a visitor, to have uttered as his last earthly words, 'Give Dayrolles a chair.'

This was the standard of etiquette that new adventurers in this promised land of consummate manners were challenged to attain.

Visits of condolence should be paid within a short period of the melancholy event, and your conversation should show that you really sympathise with your friends in their affliction. Be careful not to wound the feelings by any attempts at cheerfulness, and do not open afresh the fountain of tears by allusions to the lost one.

A Manual of Etiquette for Ladies (1855)

The ladies of a bereaved family should not see callers, even intimate friends, unless they are able to control their grief.

The Book of Etiquette LADY TROUBRIDGE (1926)

As soon as a death has taken place it is the duty of the head of the family, or some responsible member of it, to write and inform relatives and friends, and again when the day and the hour of the funeral are settled they must be told.

Etiquette for Women G.R.M. DEVEREUX (1919)

The announcement of a death in the obituary columns of the newspapers, together with the funeral arrangements, is an essential, as it is only by this means that those outside the immediate family circle learn the sad news.

The Book of Etiquette LADY TROUBRIDGE (1926)

Letters of condolence should at once be written on receipt of the tidings. These are always difficult to write. Gushing and platitudes should be strictly

avoided, and it is in the worst possible taste to speak of
the loss as a 'happy release'.

Etiquette Up To Date
CONSTANCE BURLEIGH (1925)

Tradition of a 'handsome funeral' still lingers amongst
the poor, and so strongly that many of them subscribe to
societies which return capital with interest at death, for
the sole purpose of being buried 'right' – that is, with
great display. It often happens that a widow in the
poorer classes leaves herself penniless and in debt because
of her lavish expenditure upon her husband's funeral.

The Book of Etiquette LADY TROUBRIDGE (1926)

The fashion for wearing handkerchiefs which are made
with a two inch square of white cambric and a four inch
border of black, may well be deprecated.

Manners and Social Usages
MRS JOHN SHERWOOD (1884)

Unless you are very intimate, it is an evidence of better
taste to leave a card than to intrude upon private sorrow.
Should you be so nearly related as to render a personal
visit necessary, take care to appear in a quiet dress, and
if the occasion be the death of a person even slightly
related to you, go in mourning.

Complete Etiquette for Ladies (1900)

As a rule the ladies of the family do not leave the house before the funeral, dressmakers and milliners being summoned if orders are to be given for mourning.

The Book of Etiquette LADY TROUBRIDGE (1926)

There are those who advocate the abandonment of crape in deep mourning, pointing as an example to a Royal lady who refused to wear it when suffering bereavement some time ago. This is no valid argument so far as the general public are concerned. The use of crape is to announce to friends and acquaintances and others that our loss is so recent and our grief so acute that we must be excused from ordinary conversation.

Manners for Women MRS HUMPHRY (1897)

The older custom was that bereaved families supplied to mourners and bearers crape scarves, long hatbands, and other signs of grief, but this has long ago fallen into disuse.

Cassell's Book of Etiquette (1921)

With regard to jewellery, diamonds and pearls are frequently worn with very deep mourning.

Etiquette for Ladies (c.1920)

No one except a very tactless person would presume to ask a friend in deep mourning for whom she was wearing it.

Good Manners for All Occasions
MARGARET E. SANGSTER (1921)

Widows wear mourning for two years, at least that is the regulation time; but many widows wear it for three, or even longer. For a year, too, widows should not give nor accept invitations nor go into society.

Etiquette for Women G.R.M. DEVEREUX (1919)

In the period of duration of mourning there have of late been radical changes. Widows' weeds used to be worn for a year and six months. It was then reduced to a year and a month, the vulgar reading of which was a year and a day ... It is followed by three months of half-mourning, the changes of which are quite as radical as those of previous periods. In old days only grey, white lavender, and a certain shade of violet were permissible.

Manners for Women MRS HUMPHRY (1897)

Court Mourning when enjoined is imperative, the orders respecting which are minutely given from the Lord Chamberlain's office and published in the official Gazette ... When the order for general mourning is given on the death of any member of the Royal Family, the order applies to all, although it is optional whether the general public comply with it or not.

Manners and Rules of Good Society (1912)

The question of black gloves is one which troubles all who are obliged to wear mourning through the heat of summer. The black kid glove is painfully warm and smutty, disfiguring the hand and soiling the handkerchief and face.

Manners and Social Usage
MRS JOHN SHERWOOD (1884)

A girl does not wear mourning for her fiance except under very special circumstances, such as his death on the eve of the wedding.

The Book of Etiquette LADY TROUBRIDGE (1926)

A man does not observe the etiquette of mourning so strictly as his wife and daughter. But it is necessary to mention that it is bad form for him to resume his social life for at least two months.

The Book of Etiquette LADY TROUBRIDGE (1926)

At the time appointed, which is generally in the afternoon, those who are invited to attend the funeral proceed to the house. The invitations usually extend only to the particular friends of the deceased, and the family doctor and lawyer.

They assemble in the dining-room or the library, waiting until the undertaker and his assistants are ready. The ladies of the house do not appear until the mournful procession is ready to start, when they go direct from their own rooms to the mourning-coaches which are appointed to convey them.

Cassell's Book of Etiquette (1921)

In the past it was not usual for ladies to attend funerals. Queen Victoria changed this custom.

Cassell's Book of Etiquette (1921)

No longer is it permissible to follow the curious old-fashioned custom of sending an empty carriage to drive in a funeral procession in token of the respect which the owner was prevented from showing by appearing in person.

Encyclopaedia of Etiquette EMILY HOLT (1901)

It was the sweet old English custom for each mourner to carry a sprig of rosemary.

History of the Book of Common Prayer
LEIGHTON PULLAN (1900)

When the first part of the service is concluded the clergyman proceeds to the grave, followed by the bearers and the mourners in the same order that they entered church. When the last sad rite is ended, the group breaks up and disperses irregularly.

Cassell's Book of Etiquette (1921)

Veils act as screens between ravaged faces and the eyes of passers-by.

Vogue's Book of Etiquette (1923)

The elaborate mourning expressed by long crape veils … once so general, is now regarded as ostentatious.

The Book of Etiquette LADY TROUBRIDGE (1926)

People with weak eyes or lungs must not wear a heavy crape veil over the face. It is loaded with arsenic, and is most dangerous to sight and breath.

Manners and Social Usages
MRS JOHN SHERWOOD (1897)

Upon their return from the funeral the family should find the blinds of the house drawn up and all outward signs of sorrow removed. The furniture should be in its usual order, and everything connected with the funeral should be out of sight. The members of the family should be greeted with nothing on their return that would possibly give cause for fresh sorrow. A considerate friend or relative should stay behind to attend to these details. It is not enough to leave them to a servant.

The Book of Etiquette LADY TROUBRIDGE (1926)

Only the family return to the house. The Will is then read by the family lawyer in the presence of them all.

Cassell's Book of Etiquette (1921)

There is still much to be done in the way of funeral reform; the passage of the body to its last resting-place is still invested with too much pomp of melancholy and ostentation of grief. But of late years it cannot be denied that a wiser more truly devout spirit has prevailed, and the hearse and its nodding plumes, — and all the ghastly 'pageantry of death', are rapidly giving place to more cheerful appurtenances.

The Glass of Fashion
THE LOUNGER IN SOCIETY (1881)

Memorial Brasses: A narrow strip, not more than perhaps four inches wide, with a plain continuous text upon it, may fitly be placed, simply as a record, not an advertisement — but only placed where it does not meet the eye of one entering the church.

Manual of Church Decoration and Symbolism
ERNEST GELDERT (1900)

Bibliography

Here is a selection of the original reference books used for this anthology.

ANON., *Complete Etiquette for Ladies: A Complete Guide to the Rules and Observances of Good Society* (1900)

ANON., *Etiquette for Ladies and Gentlemen* (c.1870)

ANON., *Hints on Etiquette and the Usages of Society*, 3rd ed. (1836)

ANON., *The Complete Etiquette for Gentlemen. A complete guide to The Table, The Toilette, and The Ball-Room* (c.1878)

ANON., *The Complete Etiquette for Ladies and Gentlemen. A Guide to the Observancies of Good Society*, new ed. (c.1920)

ANON., *The Habits of Good Society. A Handbook of Etiquette for Ladies and Gentlemen* (1859)

ANON., *The Standard Cyclopedia of Useful Knowledge, Vol V* (1896)

ARMSTRONG, LUCIE HEATON, *Etiquette-Up-To-Date* (c.1924)

Beeton's Complete Letter-Writer for Gentlemen (c.1860)

BURLEIGH, CONSTANCE, *Etiquette Up To Date* (1925)

CENSOR, *Don't: A Manual of Mistakes and Improprieties more or less prevalent in Conduct and Speech* (c.1880)

DEVEREUX, G.R.M., *Etiquette for Women: A Book of Modern Modes and Manners* (1902 and 1919)

LADY GROVE, *The Social Fetich* (1907)

Home Chat – Vols. One and Two (1895)

MRS HUMPHRY, *A Word to Women* (1898)

MRS HUMPHRY, *Manners for Men* (1897)

MRS HUMPHRY, *Manners for Women* (1897)

MRS HUMPHRY, *What Shall I say? A Guide to Letter Writing for Ladies* (1898)

A LADY, *A Manual of Etiquette for Ladies: or, True Principles of Politeness* (1855)

LANE, HARRIET, *The Book of Culture* (1922)

LEVITT, DOROTHY, *The Woman and the Car* (1909)

THE LOUNGER IN SOCIETY, *The Glass of Fashion – Social Etiquette and Home Culture for Ladies and Gentlemen* (1881)

M.C., *Everybody's Book of Correct Conduct* (1893)

THE MAN IN THE CLUB-WINDOW and A MATRON, *The Habits of Good Society: A Handbook of Etiquette for Ladies and Gentlemen* (1859)

Martine's Hand Book of Etiquette and Guide to True Politeness (1865)

MASON, CHARLOTTE M., *Home Education: A Course of Lectures to Young Ladies* (1899)

A MEMBER OF THE ARISTOCRACY, *Manners and Rules of Good Society – or Solecisms to be Avoided* (1912)

NICHOLSON, W., *How to be a Lady: A Book for Girls – to which is added The Lady's Book of Manners* (c.1880)

SENN, C. HERMANN, MBE, FRHS, *The Art of the Table* (1923)

LADY TROUBRIDGE, *The Book of Etiquette. The Complete Standard Work of Reference and Social Usage* (1926)

TURNER, EDWARD (Ed.), *The Young Man's Companion or Friendly Advisor* (1866)

A WOMAN OF THE WORLD, *Cassell's Book of Etiquette* (1921)

The World of Fashion (1828)

The World's Work (1913)

The author wishes to thank all these admirable Ladies and Gentlemen for their strict observance in delicate matters of behaviour.